D0853345

DANCING *at the* EDGE *of* LIFE

DANCING *at the* EDGE *of* LIFE

A MEMOIR

GALE WARNER

with DAVID KREGER, M.D.

foreword by DR. BERNIE SIEGEL

NEW YORK

The author gratefully acknowledges permission from these sources to reprint the following: Excerpt from *I and Thou* by Martin Buber, translated by Walter Kaufmann. Translation copyright © 1970 by Charles Scribner's Sons. Reprinted with the permission of Scribner, a Division of Simon & Schuster; excerpt from *The Prophet* by Kahlil Gibran, copyright © 1923 by Kahlil Gibran and renewed 1951 by Administrators C.T.A. of Kahlil Gibran Estate and Mary G. Gibran. Reprinted by permission of Alfred A. Knopf, Inc.; excerpt of "The Holy Longing" by Goethe, translated by Robert Bly, from *News of the Universe*. Copyright © 1980, 1995 by Robert Bly. Reprinted with permission of Sierra Club Books; excerpt of "Spring and All" by William Carlos Williams, from *Collected Poems 1909–1939, Vol. I.* Copyright © 1938 by New Directions Pub. Corp. Reprinted by permission of New Directions; excerpt from *Touching Peace: Practicing the Art of Mindful Living* by Thich Nhat Hanh, copyright © 1992. Reprinted with permission of Parallax Press, Berkeley, California; "Fidelity" by D.H. Lawrence, from *The Complete Poems of D.H. Lawrence* by D.H. Lawrence, edited by V. deSola Pinto & F. W. Roberts. Copyright © 1964, 1971 by Angelo Ravagli and C. M. Weekly, Executors of the Estate of Frieda Lawrence Ravagli. Used by permission of Viking Penguin, a division of Penguin Books USA Inc.

An exhaustive effort had been made to locate all rights holders and to clear reprint permissions. If any required acknowledgments have been omitted, or any rights overlooked, it is unintentional. If notified, the publisher shall use its best efforts to ensure that proper credit will appear when appropriate in all future editions of this book.

 For information address Hyperion, 114 Fifth Avenue, New York, New York 10011.

Library of Congress Cataloging-in-Publication Data
Warner, Gale.

Dancing at the edge of life : a memoir / Gale Warner with David Kreger : foreword by Bernie Siegel. 1st ed.

p. cm.

ISBN 0-7868-6392-7

1. Warner, Gale—Health. 2. Lymphoma—Patients—Massachusetts—Diaries. 3. Warner, Gale. I. Kreger, David. II. Title.

RC280.L9W37 1998

362.1'9699446'0092—dc21

[B] 97–38597

CIP

Designed by Jill Gogal

FIRST EDITION

10 9 8 7 6 5 4 3 2 1

Fate is encountered only by him that actualizes freedom . . . [H]e that puts aside possessions and cloak and steps bare before the countenance—this free human being encounters fate as the counter-image of his freedom. It is not his limit but his completion; freedom and fate embrace each other to form meaning; and given meaning, fate—with its eyes, hitherto severe, suddenly full of light—looks like grace itself.

—Martin Buber, *I and Thou*

Foreword

As I sat down to read *Dancing at the Edge of Life*, a program about the history of the Olympic Games was on television. Great feats of endurance, skill, and courage were displayed and commented on. The closing event of the program showed a marathon runner entering the stadium, in the darkness, hours after everyone else. Obviously injured, displaying bandages on his legs, and totally exhausted, he struggled to finish. The announcer stated, "This is a performance that gives meaning to the word *courage*." After crossing the finish line the athlete was asked why he bothered to finish the race. He said, "I did not come to start the race but to finish it."

If I had to sum up Gale's life and this book, those are the words I would choose.

I cannot write a conventional foreword to so moving a book and so real a life. I would end up writing another book. There is just so much wisdom in it that I would want to point out to you. I can only tell you it made me laugh and cry and appreciate life even more.

Gale shares the truth about life that we all so desperately need to be aware of. Read and learn so your mortality can be appreciated and you don't postpone your life until someone tells you you are going to die.

What are some of her teachings? How to use the Holy Shit (my expression) that life presents us with as fertilizer. Gale talks about the compost and how we even deny death by disposing of our potential compost—out of sight, out of mind—but it doesn't really work. She teaches us how to use and learn from our pain. How to find the personal meaning in our disease and our life.

All we are asked to do is live and die. So many of us die without ever having lived, but not so with Gale. She asks the questions and feels the feelings. After you have read this story you will find life easier to understand. All the questions about failure, guilt, blame, God, evil, and more are explored as a part of her experience.

Why do young people get sick and die? Because it isn't a perfect world. Why isn't it? Because we are participants in creation, as Gale realized. What is evil? A disease? No. Evil is to not respond with compassion to the individual who is suffering or to the planet Gale so worried about.

She shared how she had wanted to write many books. Well, I think she has said it all and is aware of that now. She leaves us with more work to do. Read her words and join her in doing God's work. As she and God know, the grace comes unbidden.

The grace is available to all. So is the wisdom and beauty of Gale's life. Read it and feel the passion of life and then live and heal yours. The book is Gale's gift to you. Your life is your gift to use wisely in the name of creation.

When you are moved to tears remember that grief is a part of life, and just as Gale used her pain to create and know herself she would not want us to grieve forever. Her sense of humor makes that very apparent. Gale is now part of the beautiful light and I ask that you don't let your tears extinguish her candle. Let her light guide you out of the darkness we all face and learn from.

Under pressure, charcoal becomes a diamond. This book is just such a treasure.

Bernie Siegel, M.D.

PART ONE
initiation

November 29, 1990

Some part of me must have known all along, for I feel prepared for this, and it all seems quite believable.

Today I will go to the Dana-Farber Institute for a biopsy, bone marrow exam, and other tests. Yesterday, I went to Salem Hospital for a chest X ray. It only took a minute or two. Then Dr. Cooper surprised us by arriving in the radiology department and ushering us into a room. He closed the door. "There's an abnormality on the X ray," he said, "something unusual in the anterior mediastinum." He said it so quickly that I didn't really get it. But my husband David, who is a doctor, turned pale. He and Dr. Cooper kept talking in medical jargon. Then there was a pause. David swallowed hard and said, "I think we're a bit in shock." Only then did I realize that they'd found something serious.

Dr. Cooper showed us the X-ray films. It did not take a trained eye to see it—a large white mass, the size of my fist, above the left lung, hanging out into the chest cavity. "Now, *something's* there, but we don't know what it is," Dr. Cooper continued. "It could be just an infected node, or a benign tumor." Within minutes he had arranged for an appointment with the chief of oncology later in the afternoon.

"I don't have to tell you about the importance of seeing beyond the present to a happy ending," Dr. Cooper said. "But I want you to keep remembering that after this morning there will be answers and a treatment. You're walking, talking, smiling, and you will be for a long time yet."

We left and walked to the car. "He's reassuring me by telling me I'm still alive. That doesn't sound too good."

"I'm scared," is all David said.

"Then I think I should drive." I took the keys, and at that precise instant, I began to recover. I felt a blast of cosmic humor. I have a tumor the size of an avocado in my chest, and *I'm* driving home! Then David began to cry. He needed to talk to someone, immediately. When we got home, he called our friend Rick, and I went upstairs to lie down. I wondered at my calm. "This is not a bad dream," I said aloud. In fact it didn't feel like a dream at all, just another morning in my life, and an achingly beautiful one at that—blue sky, warm still air, sunshine, the earth warm and beckoning. I thought of the Sioux phrase: "It's a beautiful day to die."

When people hear they have cancer, they suddenly notice the sweetness of the air, the beauty of trees, the tenderness of loved ones, and are seized by wonder. "How is it I have been living and not truly seeing this before?" But I have no sense of having let life slip by, no regret for the dreams I did not follow. I will keep loving as before, writing as before. The marsh is as beautiful today as it was yesterday. It is not a hundred times more magnificent, simply as beautiful as it has always been.

David came upstairs, looking shaken. We held each other and cried. I thought: Yesterday I loved this man, and today I love him just the same. "I *would* like to write my novel," I said, "and have a baby." We went down our street to the beach and watched the white gulls, the wind weaving patterns in the sand, the red and black tide pools.

"Can you imagine what cancer is going to do for my career?" I said to David. "I could write a best-selling story of survival, get on all the shows. We're talking 'Oprah.' We're talking NPR. If those doctors don't find a malignancy, my whole career is shot!" I began to dance and pantomime a little comedy skit ending with the rap song David wrote after he studied with Bernie Siegel:

> Anticipate miracles, mobilize immunity
> Change your life, and join the community!

For so long, I've been training myself to view death as part of life. Recently, I have been meditating on Ragana, the wild dark goddess of destruction and renewal, and thinking hard about what it would mean to build temples of worship to a goddess of death and regeneration. It looks like I'll be continuing this exploration, in a big way.

When I led workshops for social activists in Moscow and Leningrad, I helped them get in touch with the possibility that they could die of cancer caused by radiation or toxic chemicals. Now there is a chance that I myself am a victim of Chernobyl. I have been attuning so closely to the Earth that I may be manifesting in my own body what is in hers. Humanity living out of balance with nature is her cancer, a fast-growing malignancy, life-threatening yet curable. It fits. It is one answer to the question "Why me?" Perhaps I have tuned in so deeply, so wholly, that I've become as sick as the planet. And in the process of healing myself, I will help heal the world.

"You know," I said to David, "With this news, I'm no longer a sick person lying around in bed waiting to get well. I'm a person with a goal and lots of work to do. Who says I can't run through the waves with cancer? Who says I can't dance and sing?" I rolled up my pants and walked into the ocean's living waters, carefully washed my face three times, and blessed my eyes, nose, lips, ears, mind, heart, and spirit. Confidence entered me, and strength. I felt deeply happy, and we stopped to collect some sprigs of bittersweet among the tidal rocks.

We drove back to Salem Hospital. The oncologist—Joseph Halperin—was very kind, very compassionate. He gingerly tried to gauge our emotional state. "This must have come as a big shock to you," he said, with an inquiring look. He immediately found some surface nodes to biopsy and called in a pathologist. He sensed David's guilt—"Why didn't I, a doctor, think of this earlier?"—and they had a rather lengthy discussion of how impossible it is to be both the doctor and the spouse.

I was feeling a bit left out so I chimed in, "It seems to me I haven't been sick that long." Dr. Halperin agreed, and assured us that the delay in diagnosis would not affect the treatment. My aching shoulder had been dogging me on and off for months—I had thought I pulled a muscle doing yoga and somehow kept reinjuring it. David said that a few weeks ago—after someone pointed out that my right shoulder was higher than my left—he imagined a large tumor under my shoulder blade pushing up my shoulder, but quickly dismissed it as unthinkable. I began to feel genuinely sick only about four weeks ago, and if you ask me, the diagnosis came pretty quickly given how confusing the symptoms were. The main problem four weeks ago was stomach cramps, which led us to Dr. Cooper, a gastroenterologist. David and I thought I had picked up a bug in Russia; Dr. Cooper thought I might be pregnant and checked twice to be sure. When all the various tests were negative, he had a surgeon examine me, but the surgeon seemed a bit mystified and understandably didn't see any connection between my stomach cramps, an "old shoulder injury," and a bizarre intermittent shooting pain in my left eyebrow. It turned out to be Mom who solved the mystery. A couple days ago, I told her about my slight cough that gets worse when I change position. The chest X ray revealing the tumor was her idea.

The pathologist made three sticks in my neck to get a few drops of lymphatic fluid. Then Dr. Halperin walked in with four cups of orange fluid for me to drink before the CAT scan and placed them on the table as if he were serving tea.

"I feel like I'm wearing a scarlet C on my chest, and the entire hospital staff is here to serve my every need."

"Yeah," said David. "You're the reason they have these big fancy machines. You're the reason they went through all their training." We had an hour before the CAT scan and I suggested we go outside.

We wandered to a lovely grass-fringed granite knoll, and a kestrel glided by in the wind and sunshine—it was such a good omen I could not even speak about it. After a peaceful silence, I wondered aloud how I should give people the news. "My parents have few real fears left in the world," I said, "except for a child dying prematurely. I want to make it as easy for them as I can."

We walked back and had to wait a long time for the CAT scan; then suddenly, exhaustion hit me. The scan was difficult and surreal. It was hard to take deep breaths without coughing, and harder still to hold my breath for very long. In that position—arms over my head—my back and shoulders ached piercingly. Finally the ordeal ended.

When we returned, Dr. Halperin was ready for us. From the CAT scan, it appeared the tumor and swollen lymph nodes were all in the upper chest. The needle aspiration indicated that it was lymphoma—a non-Hodgkin's, "rather aggressive" lymphoma. Although I'd had all day to prepare, my heart pounded at the sound of it.

The next steps: a surgical biopsy, a gallium scan to establish a baseline for comparison, a bone marrow exam. Dr. Halperin said we could do some things at Dana-Farber Cancer Institute in Boston and some things closer to home in Salem. He made an appointment for us to meet Dr. "Tak" Takvorian, a lymphoma specialist at Dana-Farber, and it seemed we had the best of all possible worlds: two "family" oncologists in Salem to be advocates, and access to one of the finest cancer centers in the world.

When we got home, I opened Kahlil Gibran's *The Prophet*, and read the passage on death aloud. The last five phrases are the most beautiful of all:

> For what is it to die but to stand naked in the wind and to melt into the sun?
> And what is it to cease breathing but to free the breath from its restless tides, that it may rise and expand and seek God unencumbered?
> Only when you drink from the river of silence shall you indeed sing.
> And when you have reached the mountain top, then you shall begin to climb.
> And when the earth shall claim your limbs, then shall you truly dance.

Deeply comforted, I put the book aside and slept. When I awoke I pictured our doctor friend Rick standing in his clinic facing the window and crying after hearing the news. This loosened my own tears, and I cried, too. Then I sat at my desk to write.

I thought for awhile about whether to start a fresh notebook or not. It seemed a bit melodramatic, given that one of the overriding insights is that there is no sharp break in my life between today and yesterday and the day before. Each day comes with what it has to offer and goes away quietly. I am not fundamentally different today: I am still Gale, my life is still my life.

My first reaction this morning was to think about my feelings on the plane coming home from the Soviet Union two months ago: how robustly healthy I had felt, and how fulfilled. I had looked ahead to the rest of my life with a satisfied sense of many missions well done and well completed. How clearly I had felt that my thirty years so far had been good ones, that I had had so many riches and blessings heaped on me, so many piles of experiences, any one of which would have made the trip to Earth worthwhile. And how I had articulated to myself, then, that from here on it was really gravy, it was all extra. I had written in my journal that the plane could go down and I'd still have nothing but gratitude and blessed feelings about my life.

How lucky am I, to have had those strong feelings and insights *before* all this—so I can be confident of how genuine and real they are.

So. I have cancer. I have a tumor in my upper chest, large and fast-growing. It is a form of lymphoma—exactly what type, we are not sure yet.

I wrote much of the day while David made arrangements by phone for our visit to the Cancer Institute. Dr. Takvorian said right away, "I don't hear anything horrible or anything that's not curable." David pushed hard to schedule all the procedures on Friday. Tak said that would be hard, but a few hours later he called, "I don't really know how but I managed to do it."

"Miracles are already starting to happen," I said cheerfully.

The first thing I noticed about Tak was the large blue button he was wearing that said DON'T PANIC. He was very clear and calm, and he suggested we do the bone marrow exam right away. He told me exactly what he was doing and how much it would hurt, just enough in advance that it wouldn't be a surprise. David was there to hold my hand and stroke my hair. "Now, I'm going to pin you to the table,"

Tak said, just before he went into the bone. The pain was short, intense, and quickly over.

After the bone marrow exam, Tak methodically covered the spectrum of possible types of lymphoma, but cautioned, "I don't know what you have until we get the pathology report." At the end of our talk, he said there are only a few cases of women recovering their fertility after having lymphoma and receiving chemotherapy.

Can I weave a web of light around my ovaries? Can I imagine one of the beautiful little snakes I used to send scuttling in the grass now coiling protectively around my eggs?

I was dispatched to nuclear medicine to get an injection for the gallium scan and David and I began talking about fertility right away. "If we decide to, we'll adopt," said David, and we both felt something mysterious had just been explained to us. We had never been able to visualize me with an infant, and now, in a curious way, the responsibility for making a decision had been taken from us.

The gallium injection was easy, although I noticed heavy lead casing around the syringe. One drop fell on a napkin, which the technician carefully folded and placed in a metal box. Low-level radioactive waste. I once wrote an article about how problematic it is to dispose of it and now I'm generating it. "That drop alone would set off a Geiger counter," the technician said. David teased that I would be ringing shoplifting detectors in bookstores for the next few days.

This was also the day we released concerns about money. Obviously we are going to go way over our $5,000 deductible, so there's no point in worrying about how much each procedure costs. Just before Tak took the bone marrow punch he'd said, "I don't know what kind of insurance you guys have, but this little procedure will run you a cool few thousand." We blanched when we realized how close we had come to not being insured at all—our policy just became effective a few months ago, and before that we were uninsured for more than a year.

In the waiting room at ambulatory procedures, I heard my surgeon was delayed. If he was too late, the nurses would go home and my biopsy would have to be rescheduled. An outrageous idea came to me: "I feel like trying to bribe the secretary and the nurses with chocolate chip cookies to get them to stay." "Do it!" said David. "What can you lose?" I found the surgeon's secretary in her cubicle and blurted out my offer. She smiled anxiously and said, "We're doing all we can." Fifteen minutes later she'd found another surgeon to examine me. A few minutes after that, my doctor showed up. I was so relieved. To miss this biopsy would mean a week's delay in diagnosis and therefore in treatment. Every instinct in my body was saying *hurry*.

I gave my amethyst necklace to David for safekeeping. I had been told: local anesthetic, twenty-minute procedure, no big deal. But there was one thing I forgot. My back. At first it was all merely interesting. The little whirring of the cauterizer, the blue fanned cloth drawn like a drape over my face. Then the tumor began pressing on the nerves in my back, and that in turn set off the muscles in my face and jaw. It was pure agony. I started breathing hard, fighting down panic. "The surgery doesn't hurt at all, but my back goes into spasms," I explained. "Could you massage me?" The nurse did her best, but I began to feel hot and sweaty. My hands moved around, trying to find something to clutch. Only her rubbing of the sore spot on my back kept me from screaming out loud. When I began to hyperventilate, she brought me a paper bag to breathe into. I knew they hadn't found a node to biopsy and altogether I was much too awake.

"See anything yet?" I knew it was bad taste to ask questions like that of your surgeon, but I was feeling desperate. It was thirty minutes into the procedure and my back pain was searing. I could hear the frustration in my surgeon's voice as he muttered to the nurse: "I see one, but it's under the jugular vein. I have to be careful."

Forty minutes into the procedure the surgeon said, "If you can't handle this, tell us and we'll stop." I have to lie, I realized. They have to get that node. I knew this was a critical moment on my journey: whether I had the courage to endure it could determine whether I would live or not. A week's delay in treatment could tip the scales. "I'm okay," I called out weakly. "Just get this thing." As I strained to think of a way to get through it, the song "Amazing Grace" came into my head. I began to sing it in a soft, barely audible whisper, embarrassed lest the nurses hear. *Through many dangers, toils, and snares, I have already come* . . . I heard the surgeon say quietly: "That's the tumor." *How precious did that grace appear the hour I first believed* . . .

Suddenly, inexplicably, I felt the pain let go. "I think we can get to it now," the surgeon said. I felt him tugging, probing, snipping. "I think we got enough," he said. "Do you mind if I sing?" I asked the surgeon. "Sure, go ahead." And so I began to sing out loud, one breathless line at a time. *We've no less days to sing God's praise, than when we first begun.*

"That was almost a mediastinal dissection," the surgeon muttered as he finished stitching me up, meaning he'd entered at my neck but gone nearly into my chest.

I was still dizzy and breathing hard when David appeared at the door. I reached for his hand. He persuaded the nurse to run downstairs and get me Percocet, a painkiller. Slowly, the nurse helped me into a wheelchair, and David wheeled me to the car.

Back home I collapsed on the couch, loopy from the narcotic. I called Mom and spoke to her in a sing-song voice. "Oh, honey," she said sadly when I mentioned infertility. I wanted to make other calls but I felt too goofy. I was beginning to realize, however, that I would survive the pain. A few moments later, a wave of energy filled me and I began dancing on the couch. I knew that it was precisely this crazy, wacky vitality of mine that would lick this tumor once and for all.

The next day we were on the road to Maine in high spirits, with me lying in the back. Did I feel well? Hardly. Yet I was peaceful and happy. We arrived at Rick and Amy's around dark. Rick gave me a huge bear hug. "You're still Gale!" he exclaimed. It seems that everyone expects me to look different.

It is so good to be in this place where I am loved. After dinner someone began to sing "Now I Walk in Beauty." Soon we were off, chanting, dancing, rattling. I was moved to the center of the group and Rick's hand was on the tumor. A new melody came through me. I sang it again and again as the others filled in harmonies and rhythms. Kneeling, I felt everyone's hands on my body and I made a silent vow: "My Goddess, I am in your hands. I am truly your daughter now. Take me, heal me, bless me." I felt a wave of acceptance as the chanting tapered.

Later, Rick drew a bath for me and lighted the room with oil lamps. Then Amy came in to talk. "You know, many women make a big deal about having a child because it's the only real challenge they've ever had in their lives," she said. She pointed out that I have done many other things that have allowed me to find my limits and test my strength—outfoxing the KGB, writing books, rock climbing, spending weeks alone in the wilderness.

After the bath, I had hoped to have a peaceful night. Instead I was awakened at 3:00 A.M. with a severe back spasm. It took twenty minutes of massage plus two Percocets to get me back to sleep.

Back home, I took a long shower, put on colorful clothes, and brushed out my hair, so full and golden. Looking in the mirror, I felt tears rise; I like my hair so much and I know its days are numbered. I went upstairs and sat on David's lap, hugged him, and cried. Funny how there are these little trigger points. "You are sad today," a friend told me. "Most of the time, you act like someone who's just been given a ticket to the moon."

I felt the tumor pressing on me today with a new intensity, like Los Angeles suburban growth spreading through my chest. "I don't hate you," I said to the tumor. "But I will fight you. I am saying no. I am saying stop."

We went up to see Tak at the clinic. "Are you the guys with the bumper sticker that says, 'If the People Lead, the Leaders Will Follow'?" he asked. "I thought so."

The pathology report was complete, he said. We had a diagnosis. "You have diffuse large-cell lymphoma. Your bone marrow is clean and there does not appear to be any involvement below the diaphragm. You are Stage II, meaning you have it in more than one site. As lymphomas go, it's rather standard and the treatment is straightforward." Then I asked the $64,000 question.

"I understand I am not a number," I said, "but I want to have some idea of what the statistics are."

He answered thoughtfully. "The chances of the tumor responding to the chemotherapy are very good—85, or even 90 percent. For this type of lymphoma, the odds of a long-term cure are between 50 and 70 percent. In your case, those figures might be dialed up a bit because you are still Stage II—you have no disease below the diaphragm, your marrow is clean, and you have few or no systemic symptoms." He paused. "On the other hand, the tumor is big," he said, then added playfully, "or maybe it just looks big because you're little."

I took this in, let these numbers swim around in my mind. Funny, how numbers have images. Sixty percent is a rather portly, beige, nondescript male. Seventy percent has more dash, more verve—is bright green or blue, and womanly. As we walked out I felt a little giddy, almost high. Things were moving very fast.

I was starved, craving Indian food, and felt we had something to celebrate. At the restaurant, we ordered mango milkshakes: "To life," said David. I ate heartily, enjoying all the tastes, but as I was drinking tea, my heart started pounding and I felt flushed and hot. I went outside for a few minutes, but couldn't seem to stop my pulse from racing. I felt weak and had to lie down on the sidewalk to control my breathing. Perhaps I was reacting to the stimulants in the food, yet perhaps also to a visceral fear, a kind of bodily terror that my mind was, as yet, unconcerned with.

On Wednesday, we went back to Salem to see Dr. Halperin. We needed to decide where to have the treatment, and although I had been leaning toward Dana-Farber, I felt I could trust Dr. Halperin. And being treated closer to home seemed to make more sense.

Dr. Halperin pleasantly suggested we take a tour of the chemotherapy outpatient room and the oncology floor, "to ease any anxieties." When we walked into the chemotherapy room, I felt a cold sense of dread. No one was there and we saw only a collection of six red leather chairs with IV poles next to them. From the windows, there was a dull view of cars in the parking lot. The TV was on. The nurse was friendly, explaining that "people talk, or read, or watch TV" while getting chemotherapy—but I had stopped listening. I suddenly thought: I could die here, and no one would notice. This irrational thought persisted, but as the nurse took us to the oncology floor I tried not to show my fear. The oncology unit—sparkling, new, well-designed, the pride of the hospital. Yet it also gave me the creeps.

"I need to go home," I whispered to David, feeling a little sick to my stomach. As we stepped out of the elevator we ran into Dr. Halperin. He saw my ashen face.

"Did seeing the oncology floor frighten you?" he asked.

"No, I'm just tired." Some instinct was telling me *Don't come here,* and I was confused. Finally, I had to tell David. "This sounds odd, I know—but Salem Hospital isn't dramatic enough for me. I have some perverted, egotistical desire to be in a big cancer hospital with a fancy specialist." David chuckled in amazement. He had been thinking the same thing.

That night was a bad one. I got cocky and didn't take my usual pain meds, so I woke with a horrible spasm. David massaged me and rocked me until the drugs kicked in. I felt the tumor's cold black hands inside me. It was difficult to get pills down my tumor-constricted throat. I was developing a wheeze when I took a moderately deep breath. I thought of the earth being strangled by overpopulation. This cold grip can kill, yet it must be dealt with lovingly and with fierce resolve, as well. As Rick put it, "What do you do when someone has their fingers 'round your throat? What is the nonviolent response?"

By Thursday morning I was feeling better. We went back to Dana-Farber and discussed treatment with Tak. The remaining decision was when to begin—Friday or Monday? Tak made it clear he favored Monday because it was more convenient for him. "When I'm not in too much pain, Monday seems fine," I said, "but when I feel this thing pressing on me, I want to get going as soon as possible." Tak closed my chart. "Let's start tomorrow." Perhaps he'd seen a bit of the tumor in my eyes.

On the way home David stopped to pick up a package from my Moscow friends. Inside was Zhenya's healing stone, drawings from Anya, letters from Natasha, Volodya, Zhenya, and Lena. A real love-dose. Volodya's was the most moving. He said Solzhenitsyn survived cancer against great odds. A *genuine person*—underlined three times—would be able to create such miracles. "This whole process is a million times preferable to dying in a car crash," I told David. "You have time to get insights and receive all this love. What a way to fall in love with humanity. Everyone reaches deep inside and offers you the best they have."

December 9

Having cancer is a full-time job. In the morning there are pills to take, then I dance myself awake and have my eggnog, followed by a lovely hot herbal bath. There are mouthwashes and rinses, healthy foods to eat, letters to write. And David to hug.

I must not be fooled by all the excitement. Soon everything will settle down into a routine battle, a long winter in the trenches. The tedium of making the damn thing go away. But at present I'm still pretty cheerful and immensely interested in the process.

The numbers game is so seductive. A 60 to 70 percent chance of cure. Now, what do you do with that? You can't be too displeased—after all, it's better than even odds. At the same time, there's an essential difference between 60 to 70 percent, and 80 to 90 percent and it seems best not to get overconfident. Best not to think too much about statistics. But there they are—stolid, fixed, like the national debt. To be honest, I'm not really operating on a 60 to 70 percent framework, I'm operating on a 80 to 90 percent framework in my heart.

Chemo. It was both worse and better than I'd imagined. My nurse is very competent, very kind. There's something in her face that shows she's looked into the eyes of many doomed people, and a trace of it is there when she looks in mine. Her name is Pam, and she has very short blond hair. Her first words to me were about wigs, which she discussed with a serene businesslike air.

Pam is a priestess of Ragana, the old East European goddess of destruction and renewal. She is trained to face death and transformation; she competently places deadly poisons into my body. She knows their power, keeps her fingers out of their cages, yet is tender to them. I can learn much about those who served in the old Dark Temples by looking into her eyes; for surely it is the same work, and she would have been drawn to it then as now.

How powerfully the ancients understood the mind-body connection. They saw the reflection of Ragana in the creatures that came to symbolize her—tadpoles, fish, caterpillars—and meditated upon these images as a way of channeling energy, just as I am trying to do now. There's such a wealth stored in these old symbols; clumsily we try to rediscover the old wisdom. I picture the medicines as Ragana's creatures and welcome them into my body to do their work. The caterpillars munch ravenously on the tumor then transform into butterflies and fly away. The tadpoles eat up and hop away. The fish get fat and swim away. They are friendly little guys, but in swarms they eat huge amounts very effectively. Their little teeth and mouths are perfectly designed for delicately chewing away at the cancer. Picky eaters, they avoid important things like nerves and veins.

The TV was switched off in the chemo room and classical flute music was playing. There was a sense of purpose in the air. As Pam prepared to put in the IV, David suddenly got up to leave, saying he wanted to fill my prescriptions. I looked at him pleadingly and he sat down. Pam found a vein immediately but the procedure hurt more than I thought it would.

We began with a bag of glucose, then three different clear antinausea drugs dripped through the intricate little tubings. After a while I felt a fullness in my eyes. My arm grew heavy and cold; I could no longer read. It's the Benadryl, I thought; it's hitting me right between the eyes. I felt bored and hated the feeling. I had wanted to concentrate on the amulet of sacred stones David laid on my abdomen. I had wanted to bless the chemo and add to it my own healing powers. But by the time Pam began the chemo, I was too impatient and groggy to pray.

I dimly saw her put on two thick gloves and hold a large dark scarlet syringe to my arm. No dripping this one in—too caustic—she was doing it by hand.

How much longer? An hour. I remembered the surgery and thought: I can do this. Half hour. My back began to ache. I began to grit my teeth. Then, ten minutes for the last drug to be dripped in. I tried to see each medicine as one of Ragana's animal helpers. Was it the fish, the tadpoles, or the caterpillars they were putting in? At that moment I didn't care. When Pam said I was done, I was too doped up to be grateful. She gave me a heat pack for my back, and a Tylenol. I sat up and knew I had to get out of there as soon as possible, so I waved off the heat pack and walked out with David.

The next twenty hours were fuzzy. I felt I was in some kind of shrine—three glowing candles were in the room and music was constantly playing. Incense was burning. Though everything seemed distant, I felt loved and protected, in a sacred space.

Later, as I became fully awake, I found I had no control over my mind. I could not read, write, or hold a conversation; I was bored and fretful, with noticeable short-term memory loss. I was so jittery that my leg was bouncing on the floor as I lay on the carpet watching videos. One movie, *Being There*, was too slow-paced for me; the other, a French comedy, was better paced, but I didn't enjoy it. By nightfall I was pacing around the living room like a caged cat. Whitney Houston, I suddenly thought. I need to dance.

I'd been the equivalent of the living dead for twenty-four hours, and suddenly I was whirling around the room in my nightgown at full power. I danced through both sides of the tape and slept blissfully until 7:30 in the morning.

December 11

Dear Goddess, your ways are hard.
I pray that I may be worthy of these tests.
I pray that I may use this training for good.
I know you have not forsaken me.

Today an acquaintance laid an amazing trip on me. "I've known several people who've had cancer," he said. "I've been with them through their processes of healing—or not healing. It seems to me that cancer comes to teach. If people don't learn its lesson and put their lives back into balance, the cancer will kill them." His friend had lymphoma and died "because he just couldn't look at his life and make the changes he needed to make." Other friends "made the changes necessary" and recovered.

I was stunned, yet I spoke calmly. Perhaps this was cancer's teaching for some people, I said, but it was *not* for me. On the contrary, I got this at my peak. It is, in fact, an affirmation of the rightness of my path, I told him. My tumor is related to my deep attunement with the Earth and offers me a difficult and challenging initiation.

The more I thought about the phone call, the more infuriated I became. He was giving me the classic blame-the-patient message: "You created this because you don't have your act together, you're *unbalanced*, you're *defective*. You lost the race to be integrated and happy." Nonsense!

I could sense his patronizing thoughts as I spoke: "She's denying it. She's resisting facing the bad news. She screwed up her life and if she doesn't change, she'll die."

It's amazing how people project their own issues. If he got cancer, it probably *would* be a signal for him to change. I hope he learns this lesson *without* getting cancer. But to assume that there is only one possible lesson—what nerve!

I have been fretful, angry, depressed, near tears all day. I woke up with a cold sweat, pain in the jaw, and unpleasant sensations in the mouth, and worried about cold sores and a fever. I tried reading in bed in the morning, but the book eventually wearied me. I went downstairs, looked at David, and began to cry. Perhaps it's the drugs. David says prednisone, one of the chemo meds, "causes mood changes and depression." It is on days like this that I begin to believe what the doctor said: Many people will support me but ultimately this is a solo journey. It is my struggle and no one else's. There is an essential loneliness I cannot escape.

After a while I was able to summon my will, take a shower, and get dressed. I began organizing tapes, cleaning the house, cleaning the kitchen, all the while letting various waves of anger sweep through me—anger at my acquaintance and his "advice," anger at a magazine for rejecting my article, anger at my tumor for not melting away in the first three days. Thank God, no anger at David, but he had to listen to my rantings.

David counseled me gently, lovingly: "Your feelings are part of the journey, too. Feelings are not good or bad, they just are."

December 13

The cancer support group was interesting, but once was enough. The other people in the group have considerably worse prognoses than mine. I kept thinking about ending up as one of these "unlucky ones," with a recurrence, but that's hardly what I should be focusing on. David felt very strongly that it was not good for me to be surrounded by people with only a 10 percent chance of cure. Even the therapists were unsure how helpful I would find the group. "There's a lot of fear and anger here," they said, so I don't think they will be surprised by my decision not to go back.

During the guided imagery exercise, the group leader took us into outer space, past the planets, way "out there." How I resisted leaving my beloved Earth! I hated the loneliness of space, hated visualizing the "astral light." I have plenty of healing light right here—it comes to me in the sunshine, in the dance, in David's eyes. I'm not leaving this place, thank you very much. Not yet.

After the session, my mouth ached terribly and I was exhausted. But at home—fruit smoothie in hand, looking at wonderful photos, "smooth jazz" on the radio—I revived, and after dancing for an hour I felt great.

Perhaps later I'll find a new support group. For now, I think chamber music, art classes, and circle dancing are more appropriate.

It's the night before my second dose of chemo—this time I'll get methotrexate, a med that I'll get at the beginning of the second and third week of each three-week chemo cycle. I've decided the metho is a hedgehog. A bit prickly and trundly and mysterious, but a good fellow and a steady eater.

December 14

The methotrexate turns out not to be very nausea-producing. I received no sedatives, and the whole thing was a snap. I felt very little pain and said "that's the good stuff" when Pam hung the yellow bag, the color of hedgehog eyes. What a relief to know the drugged-out ordeal is once every three weeks instead of once a week.

I told Tak my cough and breathing were better and I didn't feel the tumor so much. "You look good," he said. I was disconcerted to find that I had lost three pounds, until David cheerfully said, "At least half of that was tumor!"

December 15

A very blessed evening, as we went to our first sacred circle dance only two miles away. The whole evening was a healing. I closed my eyes during much of the music and let myself be moved along by the grace of the dance. The leader, Geraldine, and I felt a special and almost immediate connection. I told her that because of my illness I was going to be doing a lot more dancing and singing.

In these first few weeks, I am learning that dance is life. It is one of my gifts, one of the ways I can welcome the powers of life into my body. "There's no bad dancing or good dancing—there's just dancing," an African soul-dance instructor told me last summer. When I dance, I feel my energy surge forward, and my vitality rises up like sap. I have discovered at least three different forms of dancing. The wild, playful dance of jazz and rock, the circle dance I do with others, and the meditative, prayerful dance I do alone in front of my altar.

I'll save some strength for the long haul, so if the first treatment does not work, I'll have some reserves. But at the moment I'm just dancing in the light.

December 17

Around 3:30 today I was drooping, feeling both restless and tired. I didn't know what to do with myself and my misery, so I went upstairs and lay down in bed. Rather than trying to read or distract myself, I closed my eyes and let myself feel the pain and fear. I took long, slow breaths, being careful to pause each time after breathing out. Then an extraordinary thing happened. In a very short time—perhaps ten breaths—I felt a powerful sense of peace. When I went deep into the pain and stayed there, in this depth, I found an amazing acceptance, a profound release. The pain was gone, and after a light restful sleep so was the tiredness. As my hands lay on my belly, I felt I was competently and compassionately healing myself. I realized this deep rest is available to me anytime I choose. The pain is a mantra; it crowds out all other distracting thoughts. For years I'd tried to meditate without success. Always my mind was filled with images and thoughts. This time, it was different. I felt as if all my life I had been hot and thirsty in a small boat, and at last I had climbed out into the vast, cool, sweet, and refreshing ocean that had been there all along.

December 18

There's no way to predict what will happen next on this wild ride! A few hours after writing in my journal, I curled under the covers to read and doze. Suddenly my temperature was 101 degrees. How could it have happened so fast? My white blood cell counts must have plummeted. David called Dana-Farber and it was clear I would have to be admitted, so I could be in "protective isolation" and get intravenous antibiotics. But there were no beds available so we had to go to Salem. I dragged myself out of bed and began to gather a few things. Several days in the hospital, constant IVs, a grueling admission procedure—this was my short-term prospect. David stayed with me, acting as my advocate. We both felt we knew more than the intern and resident, and checked their decisions carefully. I was stuck several times, and the insertion of the IV was far more painful than I had anticipated. Yet, there was something to be happy about: a private room with my own bath, and a spectacular view of Salem.

December 19

My white cell count was down to 0.180 this morning—"rather low," says David. I'm now an expert at adjusting the bed and rolling the little five-legged pole into the bathroom. The pain of the IV, I've discovered, depends on the speed of the drip-drip-drip in the tube. This fever may happen every treatment cycle—but I'm slowly coming to realize that it is not a "failure" but an integral part of getting well. So what is a little pain and boredom compared to the news that my tumor has "shrunk significantly" on my latest chest X ray!

In the meantime I have letters to write, books to read, calls to make. David brought me a fruit smoothie and I tacked up photos on the bulletin board in my room.

I am beginning to feel I own this space, instead of it owning me. If I can sustain this feeling, then I will not feel caged or confined in this hospital room I'm not supposed to leave. A lesson in inner freedom. I can be free, even here.

MIDNIGHT

My fever is going down and my counts are creeping up, but my hair is beginning to fall out. This is less disturbing than I expected. It's like the slightly awed pleasure that comes from peeling away dead, sunburned skin. I pull out whole fingerfulls of hair with a sense of wonder. This is another letting go—another release. It feels right to have it begin here, in the hospital, a kind of transformation chamber. Certainly it is better than having it clog my shower or finding it scattered across my pillow in my bed at home.

My hair is dirty and unkempt, the bangs too long. It is hardly a thing of beauty at this moment, so I feel ready to let it go. This is proof that I am not the same person as when they wheeled me in here. I am someone else. I look different, feel different. I am in Ragana's cocoon.

December 20

My fever is completely gone and I am alert and energetic. I took a shower and carefully washed my hair this morning while singing a beautiful old ballad. I felt I was washing and purifying myself to serve as an acolyte of the Goddess. Letting go of my hair means coming to Her as bald as a baby, and as trusting. I carefully combed my tresses and let tufts of hair go without resistance. Then I collected the strands and saved them so I can match the color with a wig.

I put on my purple skirt and turquoise shirt, silk leggings, and amethyst necklace. Again, an important choice: Do I accept the role of passive pajamaed patient, or wear my own colorful clothes?

Just as I was getting dressed, Tina knocked on the door. "I have wonderful news. Dr. Halperin wanted me to tell you right away. Dana-Farber faxed your old chest X rays to us and the radiologist confirms a 15 to 20 percent shrinkage of your tumor—much better than anyone would expect." I credit a good 75 percent of that to Tak's alchemy. But the rest, I am convinced, is thanks to the dancing and the meditation. That's the extra kick!

I heard the suck and crunch of the vein when they drew blood today, and I reached for David, thinking, It's not supposed to hurt this much. Next, I had an overly thorough exam by an intern looking for muscle weakness in my toes ("I'm not falling apart, you know!"). When they saw me walking around, the X-ray people said rather huffily, "You're not supposed to be out of bed!" I replied, "I can't go out of the *room*, but I can get out of bed."

The princess in the tower is weaving a rope of her long tresses so she can ride down the castle walls to freedom.

December 21

My dreams are vivid and complex. Last night I saw a beautiful mountain flanked by a sparkling forest and lake. But as I leaned out to photograph it, it turned into a scene of devastation, littered with the corpses of huge redwood trees. One enormous old tree, freshly cut and still unsectioned, was floating in the lake.

One acquaintance says my disease has something to do with being open to what is happening to the Earth and, in particular, to the upheaval in the Soviet Union. I have made myself vulnerable to all this dark, destructive energy. Hence the tumor. Oh, this New Age stuff is so tricky and so easily misapplied. "Gale was just too open, and look what happened to her." Jeez Louise. No, my tumor is a diploma. What grew it was my very deep connection to the Earth, my openness to her pain, hence the dream about the dead trees. But this hardly needs to change; it is my source of insight and power. It really is a kind of reward. But it's so hard for people to get this. Those who are afraid of the dark can't imagine cancer as anything but an evil, punishing force.

AT HOME

How grateful I feel on this calm, gray solstice morning. I have made a safe passage through the time of death. The six weeks between Halloween and solstice were the time of my tumor's greatest strength. But I am much better now. The swelling is down. "This feels like a normal shoulder!" exclaimed Dr. Halperin. The pain in my back and belly is gone. Today I will go to the ocean for a ritual of thanks and bury a piece of my hair in the sand, as a sacred offering.

December 23

I got out of the hospital just in time for us to catch the plane to Ohio to spend Christmas with my parents. But this morning tested me. I knew a lot of hair would go in the shower, but I did not expect it all to go. It was just too quick. The whole process of my hair falling out took four days, and most of it came out this morning. What bothered me most was the way the hair came out tangled in ugly mats. Once I brush out all the snarls and make some beautiful locks I will feel better. Because I was rushing to the airport I didn't even have a chance to look in the mirror before I wrapped the scarf around my head. I reached for my old blue fringed one with the tassels that swing around like hair. I am glad I have a good collection of scarves and turbans, though they are hot, and I will only put them on for visiting. I prefer to wear nothing on my head when I'm at home.

Scalp massages with oil, here we come!

December 29

Yesterday I "failed" my blood tests with a white blood cell count of only 2.1, and Tak decided to postpone chemo. Still, he was pleased with my progress. "Here at Dana-Farber we expect our patients to be stars and our results to be spectacular!" He's aiming to get rid of the tumor after only two or three more treatment cycles. I like this man's ambition.

December 31

We are waiting in the adult clinic of Dana-Farber. The parking attendant recognized us and waved us through, the volunteer with her tea and hot chocolate knows us by sight, the vital signs nurse calls me "luv" in an Irish brogue.

Today I dressed like a Gypsy princess, with my blue spangled scarf pulled through a turban and a big Indian scarf wrapped around my waist. I am plumaged in turquoise, lavender, and beige. It's a big day, a tumor-melt day, when Ragana bends over me with her strong, skilled hands, pours a brew of poisonous, healing herbs into my body, cradles my head, and soothes me to sleep with a strong and dissonant song. With her blessings, I begin the year.

January 2

What a peaceful morning—how seldom I have had any solitude recently. I danced naked in the sunshine, took a long herbal bath, read some Bernie Siegel, and took my pills and vitamins. I feel so blessedly in control of my life and health, so radiantly confident that I am getting well . . . I had not remembered how lovely it is to be alone.

January 4

Today I decided to make a solo trip to Boston to buy a wig. I playfully picked out an outrageous long, curly one, tried it on, and bought it. I miss hair, damn it, so why not go for a lot of it?

I still have my aches and pains, but I have no fears, no doubts. Everything makes sense and has meaning. I sang on the drive home with clarity and conviction. My voice has a new quality these days—lighter, less forced, more pure and supported. When I reach for a song, I take a deep breath and let it rise up through my feet.

The tumor is dying and melting at a very fast rate. It is being broken apart and washed away. And it is protesting with a mild pain, a murmur of activity. Yes, my tumor, soon you will be gone. I feel Ragana's patient fingers massaging you away, like a woman who patiently washes out a stain, a few fibers at a time.

January 12

It took discipline to eat and drink this week when each swallow was as painful as the bone marrow exam. For several days the back of my throat and top of my tongue have been a mass of red bumps.

I've surely lost some weight and I couldn't drink enough to keep my kidneys irrigated after my methotrexate dose. I kept throwing up. Then I'd just patiently force myself to drink again. Root beer, when the tummy was too frail for eggnog. And eggnog, when the throat was too inflamed for root beer. I read a book and played loud music at the same time to distract myself from the pain of swallowing. Then David brought home "miracle mouthwash"—that's really what the pharmacy calls it—and within twenty-four hours it worked. I ate ravenously today to make up for lost calories.

I was graced with a helpful call from Carrie Hyman, a sweet and funny friend who is in remission and officially cured. She had exactly the same thing, a small cantaloupe-size anterior mediastinal large-cell lymphoma that gave her back pain in the left upper shoulder and shoulder blade area. She was diagnosed three years ago on the weekend of our wedding. She gave me a full list of ways to fight the mouth sores and build up my immunity using herbs, Chinese mushrooms, and *ban-cha* tea.

Two odd dreams this week . . .

In one, I was going to get a wig, and there was Bernie Siegel, wearing bright lipstick, acting as fashion consultant. As he put the wig on my head, it began to shed. Hair started coming out in his hands. I was terribly embarrassed.

In the next dream, I was walking down the hall at school. Through the doorways I could see people rehearsing plays and dances. I hoped to audition for one of these performances, but could not make the commitment. I watched the rehearsals and then resolved to join the dancers. The performance was a musical comedy about lymphoma. On the wall was a diagram of the plot and characters. It showed a tumor surrounded by white cells, lymphoma cells, and other blood cells. I would dance the part of a lymphoma cell. I explained I might miss some rehearsals because of my treatments, but the people in charge said it didn't matter.

As I think about the dream, it occurs to me that I have been talking a lot about dancing my cancer away. This is a dream I have not yet followed. This dream to be a dancer.

February 14

Physically, I have been coping with a series of nuisance aches and pains: tummyaches, hemorrhoids, vaginitis, urethritis, sore tongue, dry lips, canker sores, runny nose, insomnia, nosebleeds, and, most of all, a general tiredness. The major problem of treatment cycle number one was a low white-cell count, fever, and frequent trips to the hospital. In cycle number two it was the mouth and throat sores. Cycle number three's distinguishing feature was anemia and tiredness. Just now I'm waiting for Tak so we can begin chemo cycle number four. I've been feeling like a real wimp and it's taken a lot of concentrated effort to psych myself up for this round. When I remember the pain I endured at the beginning with guts and good humor, I wonder why the prospect of being zoned out and a little queasy bothers me so much. Maybe I'm just getting tired. Maybe I'm getting more and more conscious of the fact that the medicines make me sick. Still, I can't get out of it. Like it or not, today I am Persephone, daughter of the Goddess, descending, once again, into the underworld.

February 19

Big news: I am clean. I am in remission. If there is any cancer left in my body, it is below the level of detection. I am as free of cancer now as I will ever be in my whole life.

This means I must only live through three more cycles of chemo instead of five, and these are only for good measure. I am unlikely to need radiation at all, so David and I can make plans for the summer. But the healing poisonous herbs have taken their toll. I feel their cumulative effects, which have thinned my skin and made me look older than my years. I awoke a few mornings ago and saw that the skin on my forearm was as wrinkled and papery as an old lady's. I began to think about Tak's advice to stay out of the sun, and wondered if we shouldn't go somewhere foggy like British Columbia instead of the desert.

Despite the booster of a blood transfusion, I am still tired. The chronic pain has worn me out. I go for walks less often and do less late-night dancing. I continue to lose body hair. My shins are fuzzy but thighs and calves are smooth. My eyebrows are going but my eyelashes are still hanging in there. Strangest of all, the hair on my head has stopped coming out and I've been left with a few wisps like a newborn. I told Tak that it was like keeping a few seed trees when logging the forest. Thanks to the loving affirmations I get of my bald beauty, I consider myself attractive. Most helpful of all were three photos David took of me wearing only white panties and a white turtleneck, which were so cheesecakey (those slim peach thighs! those sleek hairless legs! those dark eyes in the pure white head!) that I could be a Miss February centerfold in *Cancer* magazine.

For some reason it took me a long time to wear the wig. But at last I did, to round-singing and dancing last Sunday. It was nice to feel hair on my shoulders, to look completely normal, and be in a group of people without giving any impression of being ill.

Since I'm in remission, we're just zapping away "for insurance." This means a shift in my visualizations. Before, I imagined my hungry little fish, tadpoles, and caterpillars getting fat by munching on my cancer cells. What are they doing now that there's no tumor left? Before, they were working away in stagnant pools, but now they are fluttering about, investigating and cleaning, bringing in light and freshness, still doing some essential stripping down. I have another two months to go before the muddy things give way to translucency and transparency. Even my skin is thinning, my nails turning white, my veins (still faithful and strong, reliable and fast-healing) pop up to the surface and my hairless genitals reveal themselves. I am becoming lighter every day. This is what Ragana's creatures do, when their first frenzied feeding is past!

The Goddess Ragana is strong, beautiful, sexually vibrant. She is neither mother nor maiden nor crone. This is who I am—not a maiden, not a girl, not a mother—more like a shaman, or a warrior.

At a recent dance gathering in Ipswich, Geraldine asked: "Does anyone know anything about the four directions?" I raised my hand. I spoke about the four elements—air, fire, water, and earth—and the age-old notion that each element is associated with one of the directions of the compass. This idea is so ancient that it's found not only in Cheyenne Native American culture, but also in pre-Christian European nature religions, and even in Japanese poetry and Tarot. I explained that (with some variation among cultures) air is associated with the east, with spring, with the sky and eagle, and the ability to perceive things clearly at a distance. Fire is associated with the south, with summer and the midday sun, the lion and mouse, the power of will and determination. Water is associated with the west, with autumn and the ocean, twilight, and the power of introspection. And earth is associated with the north, with winter, mountains and forests, buffalo, and the power to possess wisdom and set limits. I explained that a ritual begins in the old Goddess religions by invoking the powers of the four directions, in order to cast a circle inside of which the ritual takes place.

I shared a Cheyenne idea that each of us is born with natural gifts in *some* of the directions, and that a basic challenge in life is to journey full circle around the compass, or "Medicine Wheel," in order to develop our abilities in the *other* directions where we are not naturally gifted. Later, I was approached by several people seeking guidance. How quickly and easily they absorbed these images—as if I were reminding them of things they already knew, rather than teaching them.

What a powerful tool the mystery of illness can be for learning and teaching. My last blood transfusion led me to an interesting insight. At first I felt a bit strange at the thought of letting someone else's blood into my body. It felt like an intimate intrusion. My veins, arteries, tissues, and heart filled with blood manufactured elsewhere? Then David made the point: We are really one ecological self, one connected body. In fact, what more proof of our essential relatedness could we have than our miraculous ability to exchange blood with one another? We are all one flesh. I took in blood from someone I will never see or know. It entered peacefully and made my body feel healthy and strong. Now I feel more connected with others than before. If the donor walked by me on the sidewalk and looked in my eyes, would I intuitively know who it was?

February 20

Today in the waiting room I met a fifty-three-year-old man who was diagnosed with Hodgkin's lymphoma. He needed reassurance, to be told that the treatments weren't so bad, to be told that medication is a gift from God. "Look, I've been on chemo for two and a half months," I said. "I'm still here, but my cancer's not." By the end of our conversation he had brightened, and he thanked me repeatedly.

I've been restless and impatient today—I can't wait to get out of the hospital. Fortunately the methotrexate is almost all in.

I've been sleepy, too. My blood counts are down again, yet I want so much to have energy to go to a workshop this weekend on the Goddess. I'm going to shop for a drum and some percussion instruments.

February 22

Thinking back to my first days with cancer I realize: We are as brave as we *need* to be. At first I faced down the possibility of major surgery and a bone marrow transplant with cheerful equanimity. Now here I am, moping about two more doses of chemo. Why? Because I can *afford* to lose courage now.

I've had ten chemo doses in eleven weeks. I'm a veteran. I know what platelet bags look like, where the blankets are kept, what juices are served for lunch. I've done this enough times that I get faintly sick to my stomach just entering the treatment room. I know all the nurses and many of my fellow patients. Cindy, the cheerful college student, was recently allowed to take off her mask; she still gets platelets and blood regularly. Doug was very weak at first, but he is much stronger now. There is a beautiful olive-skinned young woman who is stunningly bald; her punk boyfriend has all the hair. A calm, silent older man sits here and reads. A beer-bellied ex-soldier talks with his wife. Some of these people are scared, and crying. A teenage girl came in a few weeks ago, obviously suffering, and lay on the bed by my feet as her parents held her hand and told her she was brave. What a place this is.

My third "big" chemo dose was the most difficult of all, and in my drugged and suggestible state, I had to listen to a nurse explain all the potential disastrous side effects to a newcomer in the next bed. This was also the first time I experienced real memory loss. Somehow I managed to persuade a plumber to come unfreeze our pipes after I got home that night, though I don't remember any of it. And I made two other phone calls which I thought I'd dreamed up. Later, I left a funny message on a friend's tape: "Did I call you—or did I *dream* I called you?"

It took all of my strength to drive to southern New Hampshire for the Goddess workshop, but it was worth the trip. We played with clay and I found myself hefting a lump about the size and shape of my original tumor. I mulled this around in my hands for some time, finally twisting it into something large and ropy and intestinal-looking.

We discussed Kali, the Hindu goddess of destruction. I spoke about Ragana, and I was sure no one had ever heard of her. Then a woman told me she'd been in a healing circle for a Lithuanian friend with cancer. The whole circle had chanted to Ragana.

March 1

I picked up a pamphlet produced by the National Cancer Institute on non-Hodgkin's lymphoma which contained a fact I did not know:

"Thirty years ago few patients recovered." The brochure went on to say that new treatments had changed the outlook tremendously. But gradually, the reality sunk in: Thirty years ago, my cancer was incurable. No one had a tumor like mine and lived. This means that there are no sixty-year-old people walking around who had what I have at thirty. This means all our talk about long-term recovery is to some extent educated guesswork. A cure is such a recent phenomenon that there are no real models yet. I will be among the first generation to recover. I found this both humbling and exciting and wondered why none of my friends and family who are doctors ever pointed this out to me. I suppose they are trying to get me through the next five years, and are willing to let the next twenty-five take care of themselves.

The future is still unknown. I needn't worry that this adventure will end too quickly. What if vincristin, one of my chemo drugs, leads to some kind of nerve damage forty years from now? It's just a chance I have to take. David assures me there are sound reasons for believing that if you are five years in remission, you have a good chance of living a normal lifespan. Still, I cannot take my seventies for granted. Or even my fifties. When I think of all I can do between now and then, even twenty more years seems like a hefty gift.

When I told Mom on the phone that I'd just learned that my type of cancer was incurable until recently, she quickly responded, "Honey, don't I know it!" This explains why the news was so hard on the older generation in my family. My kind of tumor was not a good thing to have in 1960. Mom tells me that when she was in medical school, on her way to becoming an anesthesiologist, her very first patient was a young woman with lymphoma, and she died.

I had a few more insights about my tumor. In its blind, unconscious growth, it was going to kill me. But it was going to kill itself as well. So there was no future for it. There was nothing to be done except to put it out of its miserable, dead-end existence. A tumor has no separate consciousness. So killing a tumor is not the same as killing a starfish or a deer.

Still, I keep thinking of the distinction between nature's destructive force and unbridled human violence. Destruction is the creative work of the Dark Goddess, of Ragana. It is about setting limits. It is the power to which I owe my life. Violence, however, stems from arrogance and self-righteousness; it infringes on the integrity and rights of others.

There are toxic beliefs that, like cancer, will kill the people who espouse them just as surely as they kill the rest of us. These beliefs can destroy the body of the planet, and so fighting them is analogous to fighting the tumor. When we battle ignorance, injustice, greed—unconsciousness in any form—it's analogous to the battle against cancer. There is no alternative but to compassionately set limits and say "no." We can destroy certain ideas, institutions, and ways of doing things in order to save the living whole.

We must also set limits to preserve ourselves from willful attack. The fierce jaws of the lionness that protect the young—this is warrior medicine. The warrior may be provoked, but is never the provoker. The warrior looks for the peaceful way that will preserve as much life, integrity, and beauty as possible. What to do about the mentality that razes the forests or seeds racial hatred? We must eliminate this way of being like a tumor and be guided by Ragana and Kali, who destroy in order to rebuild. In nature, destruction is always committed to rebirth. In violence, this commitment is missing.

I have to admit, I've been avoiding writing about the Gulf War, which started right between chemotherapy cycle number two and number four. I've felt inadequate to write down my flood of thoughts and feelings. The most painful of all has been the simple knowledge that so many people are suffering and dying. While I don't know anybody in Iraq, invisible threads connect us. Their agony is mine. With the agony comes anger: anger at the distinctions between "American" and "Iraqi" casualties (as if one were more important than the other), between Iraqi "military" and "civilian" deaths (as if a uniform makes a death less important). And sadness at the way that television, with the help of censorship, manages to promote a heady feeling of victory without awareness of the consequences. There were no cameras in the locker room of the losing team. We have a lot more to learn from Ragana and Kali's wisdom.

Our president recently said, "A feeling of euphoria is sweeping across America." I'm not sure about that. I was cheered by polls that showed people's "overwhelming support for the war" plummeted when the questions were asked in such a way as to open the possibility of an alternative approach to war. Most people believe these alternatives were tried and exhausted, but that is not my conclusion. When the president said, before we started bombing, "We don't want to give Saddam a face-saving way out," I wondered whether he really wanted to resolve the conflict, or have a war and win it. We had a war and won, but the conflict is hardly resolved. The victory feels hollow, and I suspect it will be short-lived.

On the beach this morning, by the water's edge, I realized: The drugs are not curing me. Ultimately I will cure myself. Their job was simply to get rid of the tumor. The drugs are the crutches I currently need to walk but it's up to me to move. The next step is to let all the deep lessons I have learned in my body emerge into conscious thought.

Why do I have such absolute certainty that I will be healthy? Why have I been spared all fears? Perhaps it's because fear closes off the channels to insight. Without it I am curious, observant, alert. I am fully present in the process. I learn more and so I have more to teach.

March 12

A steel gray, mid-March, snow-flurry morning. A hilarious string of messages on the machine, half in Russian. Lots to do, electronic mail to send, recycling, closet cleaning. Gulls fly singly in a stiff wind and I sit down at last to a pot of mint tea. I have a bad taste in my mouth and perpetually dry lips, but the tea is soothing. All weekend I have been feeling the potency of the last chemo dose. My skin has definitely changed: It is pale, thin, middle-aged. When I look in the mirror, there is no doubt that I am no longer young. I see thin eyebrows, red-rimmed eyes, a slight ashiness in my complexion, like the dry brown marsh grass I see outside the window. These treatments will not end too soon. I can barely believe there is only one month to go, three doses left and "only" one big one. Already I feel myself anticipating the final flushing out of the mouth fungi, the healing of hemorrhoids, the steady rebuilding of bone and blood and skin. Some things I will always carry with me: the blue-gray scar, the heart-tissue damage, the nerve impairment that leaves one eye slightly closed and undilated, the spoor and track of the tumor's heft and weight. Initiation marks, scarification. There are white lines, like tree rings, in my fingernails from the chemo cycles. Tiny white bristles are appearing on my calves and scalp. I had a rather weak period. My weight is 102 but I still love to eat. Oh, my Goddess, this is some training.

March 17

If there were no other reason to get well, it would be enough just to go alone into the wilderness, to lie on the mountain meadows and smooth stone surfaces of the Mother, to hear the clarity of her songs. I believe that a key to happiness, wisdom, and inner peace lies in being as close as possible to the ways of plants and animals, to river and sky, ocean, rock, and stars. From these things come not only the metaphors we use to describe wisdom, but wisdom itself. If I have a garden, then I understand how pulling weeds helps other things to flourish. I understand the revolving pattern of death and seeds, bloom and harvest, and death again. I understand that not all seeds will sprout. I understand the need for space between plants. If I live close to the flow of rivers and the ways of the beasts, I can more easily find serenity among the lives of others.

The people I respect most, who seem to have lived wise and peaceful lives, all have had gardens. It is one thing to grasp wisdom with the spirit, and another to grasp with the hands.

I think I am becoming better at perceiving other people's suffering. A frightened old woman approached me on the beach and asked from a safe distance, "Whose guest are you?" She seemed so fearful and alone. I told her, with complete serenity, "I live here, just down the road." This disarmed her. I said, "Take care" to her and meant it. Yet I cannot always be open to other people's pain. I must learn the art of detached compassion or the alternative will be illness. Danite, Gail's friend who is a therapist, told me we have to open to others yet also know when to close down. At the time, I resisted this. Now I'm beginning to understand. "You can affect others, but you do not have to oversee their journeys," she said. A challenge for a woman who never loses anyone from her Christmas list, and who sends regular life updates to all her old boyfriends! Yet letting go is the lesson. The cancer helps, for it also has meant letting go of plans, certainties.

March 20

I am hooked up to the dark red bag of blood. Yes, it hurts. It is five hours of cold sloggy pain. My arm will ache for a day. The vein grasps the needle and opens wide to receive.

David brings me soup in a Styrofoam cup and places a plastic bib on my chest. "It's hot," he says. "Here, blow on it." Before I have a moment to think, the plastic spoon is at my lips, I am obediently blowing but he tips it in too soon. It burns my raw mouth and in an instant rage wells up. He assumed control, made me into an infant, and then scalded me. It is bad enough to be spoon fed, but then to be caused such injury! I have felt this rage before. It can ignite in seconds. I don't often let it out, especially with David. But I must admit it is there. As Deena Metzger says in her book *Tree: Essays and Pieces*, "If I only write the light, the book will be a lie."

I comfort myself with the thought that I am a medical miracle. With white blood cells down to a mere 0.5 I had no fever. My red blood cells are down to 26.6, so this transfusion was needed. Platelets are now creeping back up to 94, so the worry is gone. Last night I went folk dancing until almost 1:00 A.M. "Your ears must be warm," said a dark-haired man looking at my hat. I did not tell him why I was wearing it. Does he really want to know that the woman he will dance with for fifteen minutes has cancer? At the end of the contra line he wants to swing. Some stubborn arrogance in me, some pride, wants to prove how tough I am. The room spins, I fight off the dizziness. Then I march down the hall. I keep my head up. I do not like to admit weakness, especially to myself. Am I always testing myself in this way?

March 21

Equinox. A time when the light and the dark are held in balance. An unstable time, with much straining and surging, a time of swift and fierce transitions.

Exposed only to the light, all animals, including humans, go mad. We cannot live without the fertile dark. This is one of the great rediscovered truths of our time.

This is why compost is so important. If every person had a compost pile to which they regularly contributed tea, banana peels, egg shells, and potato peelings, a place in the backyard where they watched these turn into fresh and fertile dirt, we would be on our way. This is body learning. What do we do now with the banana peel and egg shell? Throw it away, into a plastic bag and out to the street. Then it "disappears." Every person in this country grows up believing in "away," in the finality of death, in a place from which nothing returns.

I woke up today thinking about Annie Dillard. Now here's a woman who, alone and completely weaponless except for her own insight, sallied forth to wrestle with the dark. She did a hell of a job. I will reread her *Pilgrim at Tinker Creek* for the rest of my life. She accepts the dark side of nature because she understands she has no choice. But she does not love the dark. She dreams of a perfect world of beauty and light, rather than this "wet ball flung across nowhere." She, too, gets muddled about the distinction between a necessary death and cruelty. She meditates on the frog that has had its body gruesomely sucked out of its skin, but she does not imagine the frog could have, in those final moments, experienced an epiphany of transformation.

March 22

The mouth, the sensitive place where the pain concentrates, gathers strength and blooms. I have had sores, irritations, yellowish patches, chronic dryness, and what my doctor calls a "beefy" tongue for more than three months. The mouth is the gateway for food and drink. It cannot be avoided. It likes to kiss and be kissed; it is a sexual place. And its sores cannot be hidden by a bandage.

Where is the mouth of the earth? In the marshes, the moist places. But with so many toxins concentrating in the marshes, in the clams and shellfish, these places are suffering and dying. So many of the clamflats are now permanently closed. Finally, last autumn, the restaurants stopped serving clams. The mudflats are like infected sores. Pain blooms first in the mouth.

Our doctor friend, Rick, tells me that a lip sore the size of a rice grain is as painful as a sore elsewhere the size of a saucer. He tells me about the homunculus, the illustration in the medical textbooks where parts of the body are drawn in proportion to the number of nerve endings they possess. The lips are gargantuan. A place of love and vulnerability. How easily the lips tremble—how much can be read from the nuances of their curves. The place of smiles, pouts, puckers, frowns. Tides flow here; pain comes out and also poetry.

The mouth can't be avoided. The places further down don't understand what the problem is. The stomach wants food and drink as usual. So you prepare your favorite tasty foods. You eat tiny forkfuls, gingerly, trying to avoid the sorest places. But there is still pain, and eating becomes a discipline—an altruistic act to preserve the larger body.

I am not fazed by fatigue, hair loss, the prospect of fever or infections. I am afraid of the sores in this tender, sacred place.

They tell me that my heart tissue is damaged. This is part of the deal. Small microscopic cross-sections are dead. But I am not worried about my heart. It is the strongest organ in my body and will keep going long after everything else gives out. The damage is symbolic, another part of the scarification, the permanent evidence of this particular initiation. The heart, too, is vulnerable and must accept some pain. But unlike the loud sores on my mouth and lips, this pain is silent and deeply held within. What living thing escapes unscarred? There is radioactive fallout in penguin eggs. No part of the sky is truly clean. The giant forests will not come back. The damage is permanent. Yet the pulse of life is strong. Strong enough for us to dance with joy.

A friend told me about a conversation between a Russian political activist and an American environmentalist. For forty-five minutes they argued. The Russian resisted hope, with the strength of innumerable inoculations against it. Yes, he works for change in the world, but not because he thinks anything will come of it. He is not working for results; rather he is trying to keep himself intact, to salvage personal integrity. The possibility that he actually might succeed terrified him, for if he believed in success he would have to believe in failure, too, with the responsibility and disappointment that would bring.

The American challenged him. The system changes slowly, but it *does* change, he said. Why should Russia be different? The Russian paused and said, "Perhaps you are right," and then recalled this fable. "Two frogs fall into a bucket of fresh milk. They swim and kick for a long time but cannot escape: One frog gives up, stops kicking, and drowns. The other frog keeps swimming and kicking until finally the milk turns into butter and he can hop away."

The refusal to believe in our ability to make a difference, this resistance to hope, is what prevents people from healing themselves. If I try and fail I will feel even more inadequate. I will feel guilt on top of everything else. So it is safer, more comforting, to leave my future in the hands of destiny, God, the doctors, and so on.

The Question faces us all. Does what I do matter? Can my actions make a difference? Is the outcome fixed?

Are we playing our parts in a movie that is written, cast, and directed by somebody else? Is it the best we can do to play them well? Or can we change the script?

In other words: Are we here to pass a series of tests, to see how well we meet the task of being human? Are the judges taking notes? Is the only real dynamic between the individual and God? If we do good only to benefit ourselves and our particular God, this is the paradigm of disconnection.

But this world is not a stage for millions of individual, disconnected dramas. There *is* a great story trying to develop, a single story that contains us all. Each of us influences it, each of our choices affects the Big Choice. It is evolving, changing, flowing, and subject to myriad influences. Infinite different potentialities can unfold. What we do sends the whole shebang teetering in one direction or another. The ending isn't scripted. This is the paradigm of interconnection. With it comes responsibility, pain, and fear of disappointment. Yet also joy. Unswerving joy. Deep, abiding joy.

March 23

It is nearly four months since I learned I have cancer. Not such a long time. Yet I can hardly remember what it was like to not have cancer. I will, in a way, have cancer the rest of my life. I have two more chemotherapy treatments and a month to go before my blood counts rise, my mouth heals, and my hair grows back in earnest. Yes, I still have one more soma/coma journey to complete. On Good Friday, no less! No one ever talks about those three days between the crucifixion and the resurrection, but I'm sure I'll be thinking about Jesus more than usual on that day.

The resurrection and return will come. I will wake up at dawn on Easter Sunday and know that I've made my last descent to the underworld. And the celebration will be mine, in a new way.

March 26

Limits. In order to boil water, you must put it in a pot. The pot sets a limit, and so does cancer. When you learn you are not immortal, that you may only have a few years to embrace life, you start doing so. The photo of the Earth on my wall shows its beauty—and its limits. It would not be the same if those same colors and swirls were sloshed all over space. In the bathtub this morning I read *State of the World 1991*. The basic ecological perspective is one of limits and finite boundaries. Remember the Cheyenne legend: We are limitless, perfect beings who must take limited human forms in order to learn, to touch, to love.

Some think of the Goddess merely as the Great Goddess. But the ancients separated her into three forms. The abundantly proliferating power of Mother Earth, who is black and fertile as the soil. The power of light, happiness, and creativity—this is the spring aspect of Laima, who cares about each soul. And Ragana, the Dark Goddess of limits, who brings night, endings, death, and decay, who sows transformation and rebirth. We fear Ragana because we have lost our place, but there were once temples to the Dark Goddess, I am sure of it. She steps forward now, with the famine, flood, and illness. She says, "Stop. Wake up. Remember who you are."

I want to see what Yellowstone looks like this year, after the fires, after it has borne her touch. I imagine carpets of splendid flowers blooming under black spears of dead trees.

March 27

I am inordinately proud of the new growth, the little white fuzz on my head. Outside my window, the tulips, daffodils, and hyacinths are also poking through the earth. I feel like exposing my head to the sun and rain.

Last night I spoke to a woman who had surgery for rectal cancer a year ago. Her rectum was removed, and her intestine was connected to her side, to empty into a colostomy bag. A Ph.D., an engineer, a Colorado River boatwoman, a mother of three. Cancer took her by surprise at age forty-three. "It's hard, when you're so young," she told me. "I expected my mind to recover quickly and my body slowly. But it's been the other way around. I run five miles at a crack. The heaviness, the weight of it, though, is still with me." We spoke about her children. I told her I couldn't imagine having responsibilities for others; healing myself was a full-time job. "The family is a welcome distraction," she said. "It takes my mind off my disease. But sometimes I feel I'm carrying all the burdens in the world." She did not mention living with the bag, and I did not ask her. In the morning I sat on the toilet, cursed my hemorrhoids, and gave thanks to God for my rectum.

I woke this morning from a long sleep and a dozen vivid dreams with puffy eyes. I was crying in one dream, and a young woman put her arms around me from behind. When I saw her face, I knew she was a witch, with healing powers.

March 28

A warm day with a restless southerly wind. It was good to hear Bernie Siegel speak last night about the physical effects of love, how touch mobilizes the immune system, how laughter and massage literally make the body healthy. I know these things, but it's helpful to get booster shots. I need to keep bathing in the ocean, to keep making love, to keep going to wild places.

This summer we will raft down the Grand Canyon. I've sent in the check. It's almost not believable. We will be on the Colorado, one of the planet's great rivers, for two weeks. It is a trip worth preparing for, training for. I now have more reason than ever to dance, to run, to do sit-ups and push-ups.

My mouth and tongue are nearly back to normal. But I notice how much slower my recovery time is. I used to have four or five good days before a big chemo dose. This time I've barely had two. I recently began sleeping well, but now I've been thrown off track again. Praise the Lord, tomorrow's treatment could be the last. I'm tempted to wear my craziest clothes, my wildest scarves.

March 31

A beautiful Easter Sunday, and I am newly arisen, grateful for this return to life. I want to say my last ordeal with chemo is over, but my tongue sticks on this word *last.* Who knows what is to come? Now that the descent is over I can admit how horrible it really was: the separation of the mind and the body—the temporary disappearance of the self. It is horrible, let there be no doubt. Yet there was nothing to do but live through it, and know today would come—as it has, gloriously, freshly, in full blue sky splendor. I am happy simply to be alive. To see the pure glistening white of a gull drop over the cliffs, to feel the sun on my thinned and patient skin. Health, dear God, will be mine again. My tongue is bright red, sore, and furry, my muscles are still weak, but my mind has been returned to me. I woke up in the middle of the night, about 2:00 A.M., and thought joyously, I'm back!

"You're a lucky lady," Tak said with pleasure and surprise. We talked excitedly about the Grand Canyon. Then I found out that this treatment can put people in wheelchairs. "You must have some sort of special karma for avoiding fevers," he added. I've been down to 0.5 white blood cells every time, and have still managed to escape infections. If they could bottle whatever it is I have and sell it, they'd be rich. My counts: a spectacular 5.0 white blood cells, 36.6 red blood cells, 116 platelets. Jesus, get this lady out of here. One more methotrexate next Friday, and a full set of scans toward the end of the month. If I'm clean, as expected, I'll have one last checkup before going West in June.

What I need to do now is play, take risks, surprise myself. The summer will be a good start. First, a women's retreat in the Sierras—something I've never done before. Then, rafting the Grand Canyon. The desert and the mountains will cradle me and heal me. Meanwhile, I am happy here on my quarry ledges, with the pines and gulls and granite outcrops.

April 3

One more day of prednisone to go. David bought me a beautiful pot of Easter lilies. And I am proud of my tulips, hyancinths, and daffodils, which should bloom in front of the house next week. Even my old bulbs from three years ago have sprouted! Along with the change of season come hot flashes—maybe from estrogen withdrawal. And though I am excited by the turning of the seasons I can feel a weariness in my bones. I pushed myself today and danced twenty minutes to *Chariots of Fire*, and felt the joy and power of the dance return. In a mere two weeks I am going to flush all these drugs from my body. Then I am going to have *my* spring.

April 4

A perfect day on the beach, on a stretch of bugless, empty, lusciously gold and pale gray sand. I ran to the rocks in the refreshing inch-deep, clear water, noticing crab claws, oak leaves, sand dollars, quahog shells, the juicy green of sea lettuce. How happy I am, my bare feet in the sand. As I look at my legs, I see a road map of blue veins through my thin and hairless skin, patterns unfamiliar to me, branching, lobate, incredibly complex.

April 5

After finishing chemo, an intense weariness set in. I came home too tired to think, fell into a hot bathtub, and went upstairs to bed at 5:00 P.M. I have been waking every ninety minutes with hot flashes, hearing one crazy bird singing in the dark. My mouth and tongue and throat are sore. The shock of chemo has not worn off even though this is my last round.

Did I expect bells to go off? No—I think it's just that until it is really over, you can't imagine that it ever will be. You have to accept it as if it might go on forever and then convince yourself that would be okay. This afternoon I felt permission to relax, just a little. And I found an intense weariness waiting underneath.

I remind myself that Pam uses needles called "butterflies" to put in the drugs. Butterflies, symbols of transformation.

April 8

After a good morning on the beach, I crawled into bed with a headache. I thought, Whoops—do I have a temperature? It was 99.8, just under the threshold considered a fever, and I'd taken a Tylenol an hour earlier. Not good. David became suddenly pessimistic. How could my counts have dropped so much in one day? I did not want to go to the hospital again, and somehow I must have conveyed this to my body. I swallowed some fluids and went to the other room to watch a video. Distraction, at times, is key. I didn't feel much better, but my temp had dropped to 99.2. I felt optimistic when I went to bed, and by morning I didn't have a fever. Whew!

April 16

Ever since I have been steeping myself in Goddess material, I have been sleeping soundly, up to nine hours a night. Last night I dreamed of a five-thousand-year-old pottery design from the Ukraine with crescent moons shaped like deer, whirling around the four directions.

I reread the Russian legend of the Firebird and suddenly realized it is a tale of the old Slavic *resulka,* who evolved from the prehistoric goddess of creativity, the Bird Goddess. The Firebird's self-sufficiency enrages the man who wishes to possess her. "I will not create for you alone," she tells him. So he abducts her and kills her. As he carries her away through the sky, she drops her brilliant feathers, her tracings, to the Earth. It is said they will bring beauty and happiness to those who find them.

Back up with the pines and granite after a rainy day. Two days ago I saw, from this place, a palm warbler and a hermit thrush. A red-tailed hawk skimmed quite close, riding the thermals from the cliff, and lolled to the north, her tail flashing.

Long ago it was said that women who were infertile or past childbearing age were the most likely to become witches. Childbearing was considered to counteract witchlike abilities. I'm sure that's true. When you have kids you are too busy to cause trouble, work magic, or challenge authority. If I am infertile now, will my hot flashes give me honorary admission to cronehood? Will I have more wisdom than before?

May 9

I have learned a tremendous amount from my painting class. Not so much about watercolor, but about creativity. These things apply to poetry and fiction as well. Be a beginner. Face the blank canvas with no expectations. The outcome is not important, the process is. There will be happy accidents. There will be guano smears. It doesn't matter. Turn over a new page. Stay attuned. In this way you learn, you gain skill.

May 16

A bad cold has laid me out for two days. I thought that after having cancer, colds would be no big deal! Still, I got through it, blew out a cup of mucus, and went on.

Slowly, very slowly, it seems, my blood counts are ratcheting back. I had a CAT scan, chest X ray, and gallium scan, and I'm still in remission. Yet a funny thing happened when I asked Tak what the chances were at this point for a recurrence. He refused to tell me and lectured me about not relying on numbers. I told him I'd just like to have as much information as possible. But still he resisted, and said my wanting to know could be a sign of "insecurity." David and I laughed; after all, Tak's a lymphoma specialist, not a psychiatrist. Tak kept saying that telling me numbers could be counterproductive (mine must be good), for if something does go wrong, I might feel especially cursed by God. Tak doesn't know me well enough to understand I would view a recurrence as additional teaching, even as a gift.

Mom mentioned my positive attitude when she first called Tak for a report. He said, "I don't know yet if she's really that positive, or if she just puts up a good front."

My optimism is so radical and challenging, it is easy for people to dismiss it. If I someday write about my cancer, I must take my readers into the dark, drag them onto the operating table, show them my pain, my vulnerability. Here comes the kicker: I *do* have pain, but it is for the Earth and for all other living things. This pain coalesced into the tumor; it is the counterbalance of love and joy.

When I think about my personal pain during this episode with cancer, it seems trivial and insignificant. I throw up my hands and conclude: There's no story here. But if I think of the marsh, the bobolinks, and the forests and the dolphins, I feel a shiver down my spine.

Helen Caldicott said, "The earth is dying." She is right. It is dying, and the cancers are spreading, and will keep spreading unless we shift onto the path of healing. This is no metaphor. This pain is real. My mouth sores and baldness and muscle weakness—these are metaphors. I am a metaphor for the Earth. Not the other way around.

May 20

The marsh is still flat and brown, but there are green edges after Friday's rain, and the leaves are exploding from their tight pinions. I can hardly remember taking so much joy in a spring. I keep careful accounts of the catkins and flowers, the unfurling buds. When the *allegro vivace,* the first rush of growth, is past, the *andantino* begins. Being on this hill allows me to watch the coiled meanderings of the streams through the marsh grass, lazy serpents flowing into the rivers, which are themselves graceful pythons. What I like best about spring is the connection between the changes in my body and the changes of the Earth. On the first of

May—the old European spring celebration of Beltane—David noticed a dark spot on the back of my head, a patch of real hair, not the feeble baby fuzz that has been with me a month. A few days later, as the new leaves jumped into the air, my hair began to sprout from the secret powers of the body. Every day I notice a new return. Stubble is growing on my shins. Pale fuzz has returned to my smooth cheeks. My eyebrows have darkened and nearly recovered in a week. Eyelashes are short but sturdy. I have hair on my upper lip and even the one stiff, aberrant hair underneath my chin is back.

Hair. Root-hair. Leaf-hair. That which gives voice and texture to the wind. The swirl of the dance. We are not meant to be stark and glabrous. We need places on ourselves that move and sway. The soft, the tender, the fuzzy. The sacred memory of fur. Oh, I lived without hair, and I am here to tell you: It is not essential, but we must have it. It is about beauty and play, and the dark luxuriant power of the earth rising through our skin.

The forests and grasses, the reeds, the flowers—these are earth-hair. Think of asphalt, cold and dead. Down with all hair removers, I say! Down with electrolysis and Neet lotions and razors for thin-skinned legs and thighs and underarms.

On the way into Boston, I pass a small patch of land with spindly trees and grasses. The landscape is washed out and weak (with so many split ends) like lusterless hair. In so many places the Earth is dead. The evidence of disease: the cough of brown smoke on the horizon, the raw mouths of the river basins, marshes filled with sores. Where are the tools of transformation—the wild, hungry power of the caterpillar, the fish, the tadpole, and the hedgehog? It was so easy to cure my own body, yet the Earth body is so large and sick. I have a fierce love in me, and so do many others. There is power in the trees, in the ravens, even in the chickadees—the power of regeneration and of healing. The tumors are large but so, by God, are we.

When I look down my legs I see a pale blue net of underground rivers, the veins, all too close to the surface. The skin has been scraped away and is vulnerable to burns, to cuts. Yet how gratefully it soaks up sun. Skin: the boundary, the container, but also the interface. Where communication happens, the place of touch. Where leaves fall down, are changed to soil, and become new leaves. Bodies have infinite possibilities.

The only true and lasting satisfaction comes from within, not from without; from process, not result. I thought that publishing books would bring satisfaction, a sense of completion. Instead, it is the equivalent of going to the store and bringing home blank notebooks and pens. Now you have the tools to begin.

You never really "finish." You just learn more and more. The happy accidents become less "accidental." You may become a teacher, but you will always be a student and humble before accidents, whose other name is grace.

As we suspected, Mom already had all the numbers Tak refused to give me. She had Xeroxed the medical journal articles and underlined the key facts in red. The numbers were good. In a study at Dana-Farber, twenty-one out of thirty-two patients with my diagnosis were in remission by the halfway point in their treatment. So was I. Of these twenty-one, only four had recurrences. That's less than 20 percent. Not too bad.

What really caught my eye were the eleven who never made it into remission. Eight of them died within a year, and the other three had active tumors. Their median survival time was eight months. Only eight months! Figure it out: No fancy chemotherapy and I would have been dead by now. Impossible to imagine, on a May day like this.

Still, for me these numbers are empowering. I feel like I wrestled an attacker to the ground and then found out he was a heavyweight champion. Wow! There is still plenty of excitement ahead. But my chances are 80 percent! Eighty percent is a solid earthy color, with green edges. It is like new plants in a garden. It is rather masculine, friendly, and hard-working. Welcome, 80 percent.

In the waiting room at Dana-Farber, a thin woman with dark, straggly hair sits in a wheelchair. Her mouth is never closed. She makes a forced, whooshing sound each time she breathes. Here is the tumor unchecked, closing off the breath, wrapping its asphalt fingers around the throat. This happens. It came close to happening to me. Only fierce, fierce love prevented it.

May 21

On the beach. A hot, windy, blue sky day. The white curved sail of a boat leaning east. Yesterday two women, a mother and daughter, walked to the end of the spit at low tide and gathered a huge bucket of clams in five minutes. "You just find a hole and start digging," they told us, their bodies damp with sand, their faces exuberant.

Native Americans must not have needed to spend much time finding food around here. Our friend Marianne went to harvest seaweed off the breakwater with a woman who collects and sells ten different kinds of it, all edible.

The days seem emptier now, more peaceful. It's two weeks until the publication party for my book *The Invisible Threads: Independent Soviets Working for Global Awareness and Social Transformation*. It is not time for new projects, but rather time for completion.

I may also finish putting together a chapbook of forty poems I wrote between 1983 and 1988. It has been pure joy to turn back to these poems and discover what in them is alive. I haven't quite followed the maxim about putting poems in the drawer for ten years, but I've come close. Some of the older ones I still like; others improved with a bit of quick editing. So I have made a collection. You can read these poems and understand what concerns me, what moves me. They are a mirror of my creative self during my midtwenties. Here are some:

GREEN HERON

The moon tugs, the sunset
loosens.
He folds himself
into dusk, amber-eyed,
a single thought.
Within his
body the blood of the marsh
whispers as it rises.

NINETEEN KEYS TO HAPPINESS

Rise before the sun does.
Drink snowmelt. Eat oatmeal.
Observe the habits of lichens.
Watch clouds. Remember
the names of plants.
Walk, or work, enough
so that your rest has bones,
but not so much
that you are too tired at day's end
to ease next to your love, read poetry
aloud, wrestle, tickle, belly-laugh.
Stalk ptarmigan. Swim naked.
Take good care of your teeth.
Spend no money. Make
no pollution. Plan books,
but do not write them.
If you must speak with someone,
let it be about the weather, or animals,
or prehistory, or the design of greenhouses.
Think about children. Go barefoot. Invent
political parties. Plot community.
Wash the dinner pot immediately.

WALDEN AT NIGHT

Nuzzling stillness, muskrat-like.
Etching a perfect wake.

Hands catching starlight
below the surface.

To keep face down
and swim freely is

faith.

Can you accept hidden
trees and snapping turtles?

Pale hands burrowing
through dark velvet.

Sudden cold current
mantling the body.

Can you abandon your
welling fear for my sake?

Sinking toes into
strata not sunwarmed.

Equally distant are stars,
birches on the shore.

Can you stroke through
darkness willing to greet
whatever rises from my depths?

MYXOMATOSIS

She would not go back to familiar
brambles and tangled stems
    but crept on the trail
between my boots

waiting for deliverance
from swollen eyes
and fur dampened to black needles
prickling every breath

Sat in the open as she had been taught
never to do
        sides pushing against rain
fear of stoats and kestrels gone
vision piercing pus-clad eyes

Clearly I was supposed to do
something
        about the white crusts
sodden feet
recalcitrant breath

She licked her side revealing
the tawny glow behind her ears

In much the way
we cover faces of the dead
I tried to nudge her off the trail
sweep her under brush
out of sight

She would not go but
huddled stiffly there
withdrawing to a deeper
stillness
        ears laid flat
eyes no longer straining

feet primly
retracted underneath
as puddles swelled around her

She would not go

A cough of wind spat raindrops on our faces
She had dared
openness
        invulnerable
in rain-soaked dignity
she waited for me
to go.

Note: "Myxomatosis: an infectious and fatal disease of rabbits, artificially introduced into Great Britain in recent years to keep down the rabbit population."

Though all the poems are good—some are very good—none, I think, are great. What is wrong with writing "good" and "very good" poems? I heard that *seventy thousand* poems are submitted to *Poetry* magazine each year. So many of us writing poetry. And all in secret, or nearly so.

Menstrual blood, flowing again. How surprised and glad I was to feel this full, dark, satisfying release. My body, and its amazing regenerative powers. No need to take medicines to kick start the system. It just began, according to its own mysterious rhythms. I am no longer an honorary crone. Perhaps there is too much youth in me yet.

May 22

Perched on a ledge above the marsh with my notebook.

I understand why my cancer is so hard for my parents, aunts, and uncles. The loss of my grandmother Edna, a few years before I was born, was a central tragedy in my family, and they do not want me to be the next. I heard for the first time, from Aunt Nancy, that my grandmother fought her cancer. She was not ready to die. She took huge experimental doses of radiation and told the doctors, "Try anything, if there's a chance it might work."

I wish I had been prescient enough, and brave enough, to ask questions. What did Edna do? What was her fight like? How did she die? My grandmother, fighting as I have, but with no fancy drugs, no Tak, no "cure rates," no Bernie Siegel, not even a clue about vitamins. In her late fifties, and not ready to die. I am the first child or grandchild to walk into this ring, thirty years later.

Just at this moment I hear the clatter of toenails on granite. I look up to see a woodchuck trundling toward me, preoccupied and oblivious. He has stopped, six feet away, only because I said, "Hi, there." He blinked, took a few more steps, stopped, and sniffed. When I said, "What message do you bring?" he threw himself around and galloped away. I swear he was embarrassed.

Blood once again, thickening, but still fragile. An ant bite on my back leaves the pooling of dark blood around it. Still, it feels as though the blood brigades are working overtime. When the reinforcements have arrived, I think I will feel a great sense of deep relaxation in the blood.

This is a dangerous time for me. I have lost the fierce protection of the drugs—their work was finished at least a month ago. I have not been strong and happy this month; I have felt burdens, I have felt pain. I am having to fight even though I'm wounded, and not in the best condition. People around me are talking about "the good news," and for the first time, I feel afraid.

May 30

Two nights ago, I dreamed I saw a giant sloth slipping into the bushes. Then a beautiful, perfectly formed lynx, tense and alert, turned to look at me from twenty yards away. Finally, I met two lions. They took human form and became a man and woman. The woman's name was Leaps, the man's was Land. Only now, as I write this, do I realize the meaning. The woman leaps, the man lands, both one smooth, feline motion. They stayed with me for some time, companionable and a little shy. The man told me the name of their tribe: Dermda. Their power symbols are the dragon, shield, and sword. But then they became reticent, as if they had told me too much. Next, someone was playing the oboe very loudly. I shushed the oboe player, and when I turned around my lion friends had disappeared.

Yesterday I was wheezing a little. David—the doctor—convinced himself that this was the tumor coming back, blocking my airway. This morning he held me so tight I became frightened, too: "Is there something you're not telling me?" I asked.

"For it to be anything else would be a long shot," he replied, and began to cry. As I lay close to him we could both hear my rasping, squeezed breath. In the early days, the tumor had made me wheeze by its sheer bulk, and I had laid quietly in his arms.

"If that's true, then I'm dying," I said. But to me this was not a fatalistic statement, only a description of a process. I did not mean, "I will die," a statement of conclusion. "I am dying" meant: Time to get off my ass, and fight anew!

However, I'm not as worried as David. I think I'm probably having some kind of allergy. In any case, we'll call Tak after the weekend.

May 31

On the sea in Islesboro, Maine. Time with my totem, the osprey, eagle of the sea. The male flew away to feed, while the female sat tightly on the nest, gold eyes ablaze. She waved her slender white wings at us when we drifted too close in our sea kayak. When we made no further moves, she quieted. But still, that fiery eye, fierce beyond recognition.

"You would think the nest would be uncomfortable, so exposed to the rain," said Rick.

"If you're an eagle," I said, "you like to be exposed."

"But the wind must make such a high nest sway and toss," he continued.

"If you're an eagle," I said with conviction, "you *like* to sway in a storm." The airy freedom of the nest, kissing the sky and the rain.

PART TWO

the deeper course, the harder tests

June 2

David called Tak to report my wheeze. Tak agreed with me that this was some sort of asthmatic hayfever, but we decided to do another X ray and gallium scan anyway, just to put the matter to rest.

I asked the X-ray tech to show me the film as it was drying, and I looked for a tell-tale kiwi but saw none. Tak says there is no cancer. He can feel no lump or swelling. In two days the gallium scan will double check, but the X ray shows nothing blocking my airway. Tak explained that lymphomas almost never penetrate airways. So I must have some kind of bronchospastic allergy, some mild seasonal asthma.

June 3

This evening, David and I sat on the quarry cliff, the place where we had decided to marry, and looked over the marsh. My breath was squeezed and raspy. I could not tell him I was safe. And yet such a calm came into my spirit as I looked at his beloved face, I said, "If this were the only evening we had left, this would be enough."

June 4

As I lay on the table for the scan, my necklace with the golden heart broke. Marilyn, my nuclear medicine technician, brought it to me as we were about to look at the scan.

"Is this yours?" she said. I took the chain and tried to put it on. But the clasp broke off at that instant. Snap! Like the shattering of the glass under the wedding canopy, an irrevocable mark in time. I am in a new era. I will never return to those old places and teachings.

Dr. Caplan, the chief of nuclear medicine, kindly got me an envelope. I put the pieces of my necklace away, and went to the viewing room to look at my pictures. I could see the difference on the chest X ray, the vague shadows leaning to the left. Bigger. But the gallium scan was the most dramatic. Four dark round spots in my chest, arranged in a little ring. Hot spots. Like Watts—like the West Bank. Rapidly dividing cells of destruction. And it was just at this moment when the full realization hit me somewhere in the belly. The universe shifted. We are not where we were fifteen minutes before.

To be told twice, in your life, that you have cancer. Reality took two steps sideways, like a crab. Five intense months of Tak's alchemy and meditating on Ragana's power, and once again the spread of lifeless asphalt in my chest. After only six weeks of rest.

We got some food and went outside. Why do I always get told I have cancer on fresh glinting days? Together we began to release all our summer plans, one by one: our friends' wedding, the desert, the mountains, the Grand Canyon. I know river rafting in the canyon would have healed me, if I just could have gotten there safely.

"There's no way to make this sound like good news," Tak said, "but it could be worse. You could have relapsed earlier, during the chemo. There are no new sites involved and there's still nothing below the diaphragm."

He laid out the plan: More chemo as an inpatient, radiation, then the bone marrow transplant. It wasn't guaranteed that I could get a transplant bed at Dana-Farber, but since I was already a patient there I'd have some priority. We talked about timing. I could be admitted for chemo the next day. "What about your book party?" Tak asked. I sighed. We had just sent out all the invitations to an event at singer-songwriter Fred Small's home celebrating the publication of my book. Tak was willing to admit me the day after the party. "I would only consider having the party," I said, "if you could guarantee that a two-day delay would have no effect on the final outcome." He paused and I knew the answer from his eyes. "Admit me tomorrow," I said.

David started asking questions about the future. How long until the transplant? When could we travel again? Should we reschedule our raft trip for next summer?

Tak decided it was time to break through our denial. "Look, there are just two many uncertainties to talk about that. From now on we take things one day at a time. Rafting in Arizona is a nice dream, but right now it's just a dream. She's too sick for anybody to be worrying about plans for next summer."

"Okay," said David, a little chastened. "We're with you."

"You have to forgive us," I said. "This turn of events is definitely a surprise for us."

Tak almost sputtered. "It's a shock! There was no reason to think this would happen—no hints, no clues, nothing to tip us off. Everything looked good. Your tumor responded quickly, you handled the chemo very well, you had a clean midcycle and endcycle scan. We thought we had this licked."

My current task could not be more straightforward: to eat each grape, each swallow of milk, each bite of meat, each brew of herbal tea with honey, and say, "This is sacred." To watch the clouds sail toward the sea and know I am not cut off from the life-surging powers of the earth, but am steeped in them. To wake saying, "This will be a good day for loving," and to sleep saying, "This day was a gift."

Every day is a god to love, to kiss, to tumble with in the grass. I run my fingers through his hair, I press my body close to him, yielding, I look in his deep gold wolf eyes. The preciousness of these days! Today is different from yesterday, and yesterday from the day before. I am afraid to lose the preciousness of Monday's god and Tuesday's god, for the god of Thursday—the first day of chemo—waits for me in the cove.

June 5

This morning, David and I went to the beach despite cold and a whipping raw wind, and ran into the freezing waves. It took much willpower, for I was soon run out of breath and genuinely gasping, but it was important to do this before going into the hospital. I will spend five days here on the fourteenth floor getting chemotherapy, and not a kiss of fresh wind on my body.

This past week was a time to finish one journey and get ready for the one to come. I had a week to hear the mockingbird sing, to watch the whale leap out of the cold clutch of the sea into the brilliant sun. A week to love David absolutely—and to sing, to shake the rattle, to beat the drum. Oh, the preciousness of those days! I am frightened by the blank pages in my notebook, and filled with fierce desire to fill them with words that are worthy of this time. Everything within me is saying, "Reach further—dig deeper—push—create!"

This week in my meditation I was told by the Goddess, "Dearest daughter, you are ready for the deeper course, for the harder tests, for things I did not ask of you before. Now that you are stronger, you are ready for Bat Medicine—the ritual death of the shaman's training, the facing of all fears, the release of life itself.

"My daughter, do not worry: I will come to you, and we will walk many bright beautiful paths together as we go into the greatest mysteries, into the holiest of places. You have chosen this, and you have *been* chosen. David has, as well. This is a journey you will take by each other's sides. You have always walked in beauty. All you have to do is keep going."

June 6

Under the dark sky last night, I danced with my reflection in the hospital window. So beautiful, the curve of the arm, the slow flowing power of the body. So beautiful, my shaved-short hair which gives me the face of a nun, stripped down to the single flame of pure devotion. The power of pure service, pure love, infusing my body with a new grace. This is my body, my vessel. This is my path. I am here! I am walking! I have taken the leap and landed, as my lions told me. I have crossed a chasm, and I am going on.

My soul was asked, on its deep travels through caves and labyrinths of the body, "Are you ready to be braver and stronger?" Deep in the body, deep in the dead seas of the tumor, my spirit said, "Yes."

"You are an initiate! We are giving you more than most—inviting you into the deeper chambers, opening the door to our secrets. We are taking you to the mountains you always knew were there but were not ready to climb.

"Did you think one petition drive, one election victory, would do it? Did you think *50 Simple Things You Can Do to Save the Earth* would do it? Did you think that once you did the easy stuff, you'd be able to put it all aside and go back to business? No, it is not a single battle. At this very moment, the Amazon forest is being burned. At this very moment, the great lakes are being soiled and cut off from their sources. At this very moment, the she-elephant wails in anguish and sinks slowly to the dusty red earth. Only fierce, fierce love will stop it."

In the sun, the IV bags full of cis-platinum are glistening, full of fire and power. I lie in bed, dazzled by morning light.

And in my tears, a beautiful woman comes into my room. She is old, yet vigorous, with a face of compassion and luxurious rivulets of wrinkles. Her eyes are wise and black, her hair shot with silver. Her dress is long and covered with a filmy veil that falls from a crescent-shaped crown. I have never been so glad to see anyone in my life. She takes my hand in hers and speaks:

"I sent my creatures to be your assistants and guides, but it was not enough. So I have come myself. I am working to heal you with the strongest medicines. I make my knife of platinum from the sacred metal body, from the hot vital depths of the Earth, and I am using it to cut the cancer from your body. It is a slow, difficult job. I use my own fingers to remove the tumor and release it to the blackness between the stars. I use my strongest herbs to wash and purify your body, herbs from the sacred body of the Earth.

"My dear daughter, I have dismissed the faithful toads, the fish, the butterflies, and the hedgehogs. I am your healer now. I am always with you, though you will not always be aware of my presence. If you need me to show myself, ask, and I will come.

"You have chosen the steepest path. You have learned courage and now you must practice it. You must walk from South to North—from will to acceptance—and from East to West—from understanding to serenity. I cannot assure you it will be easy. But you are strong, you are gifted. We will do everything to help you. Many, many beings have been alerted. A vast array of power and resources is ready to help. The Earth has always known and loved you dearly, but now she will be more present to you than ever. She has alerted all of her children, the finned ones and crawly ones, the winged ones, the two-legged and the four-legged. You will need their powers to stay strong and resilient. Turtle will carry you on her back when you are tired. Hummingbird will lead you to places of beauty and delight. Elk will carry you on his broad shoulders into the depth and silence of the forest. They are all ready to sing you songs, to tell you their names, to give you gifts. But it is Eagle and Lion, with their fierce wild love, who will go with you into the heart of the dark country, into the depths of fear. They will watch over you carefully and sleep by your side. And when you must run, lion will invite you on her shoulders. When you must fly, eagle will carry you. You have chosen the shaman's path as well as the warrior's path. You have been found worthy.

"You must know the hardest truth, which is that even we cannot see the future. We cannot tell you when you will move from the red road of the Earthwalk to the blue road of Spirit. We can only offer you this general reassurance: All will be well."

My last day to be thirty years old! David's bouquet of beautiful, raw Gloucester wildflowers stands by my bed, and Geraldine's irises are blue and golden in the window. My breath comes with a faint rush, a hushed and gentle squeeze, as if I am underwater, breathing with a scuba tank.

"Sometimes there is just bad luck," Geraldine said earnestly.

There is luck, yes. But, for me, not bad luck. "Bad" would imply I am a victim. This is not a case of bad luck—that much I know. Good luck? Bad luck? No—there is just plain luck.

My little mop of fur is growing in half silver. Maybe all my hair will be silver after this. Or gold, shot with silver. The new scars I will have! The new marks of honor!

June 7, My Birthday

Last night, I sat and talked with the Goddess. "What do you think is best?" I asked her. "Should I go, or should I stay?" She smiled at me. "It is not up to me," she said. "What do *you* want?"

"Out of sheer ingrained habit," I replied, "I want to live. I love life deeply. It has never occurred to me to want to leave."

She looked at me with dark eyes of compassion and waited for me to go on.

"But when I try to summon my will to stay," I said, "it is curious how little energy and fire come forward. I am frightened by my serenity, my acceptance. I worry I am capable of releasing too much, and not fighting as hard as I can to recover. In my thirty years I have stroked penguins, sung with marmots, run through flowered meadows, arms wide open, singing hosannas. There is no reason to live longer to learn about joy. I have learned it. But should I stay for others? Will I serve more, inspire and love more, from the red road of life or from the blue road of death?"

"My daughter," she said, "Even we, the Shining Ones, cannot know your purpose until you have lived it."

"Last time, I never seriously considered death," I said. "I passed over the fears. That was easier."

"More is being asked of you. And you have chosen to ask more of yourself."

"I want so much to rush the answer, to say, 'I choose life.' I am so terrified of seriously opening the door to this question."

"You have reason to be scared," she said softly. "It is a good sign."

I was silent for a few minutes, and felt the warmth of her hand. "You are helping me in ways I can't imagine," I said. "I want to ask you: Do you think I should die? But something in me says I should not ask this yet."

"Do not ask," she said lovingly, "until you are completely ready to hear the answer."

"Why should I be given such strong and powerful training if I cannot stay long enough to use it? Why have I become a priestess, a poet, a shaman, if not to write books and poems, to do healing work?"

"No training is ever wasted. This is the universal law."

"Then what reason do I have to stay?"

"My dearest daughter, you are walking closer to the edge of mystery. You are walking bravely into paradox. You cannot choose to go or stay by making a list of reasons. You can only follow your soul's deep desire."

"Yes." I feel her arms slip around me and smell the softness of her silver-black hair.

Today's god is early morning sunlight, catching the ribs of a vase full of thick-stemmed wildflowers—yarrow, daisies, clover. How does D. H. Lawrence describe this in "Fidelity"?

> O flowers they fade because they are moving swiftly;
>   a little torrent of life
> leaps up to the summit of the stem, gleams, turns over
>   round the bend
> of the parabola of curved flight,
> sinks, and is gone, like a comet curving into the invisible.
>
> O flowers, they are all the time traveling
> like comets, and they come into our ken
> for a day, for two days, and withdraw, slowly vanish again.

And we, we must take them on the wing, and let them go.
Embalmed flowers are not flowers, immortelles are not
flowers;
flowers are just a motion, a swift motion, a coloured
gesture;
that is their loveliness. And that is love.

All flows, and every flow is related to every other flow.
Flowers and sapphires and us, diversely streaming.

June 8

It would have been enough to wake in this clean white bed to another day of loving. But, oh, the miracle of knowing (I waited one day to be sure) that the wheeze is better! The tumor is shrinking! The tide has turned.

This has been the most dangerous and fantastic week of my life. An incredible stream of visitors came to my room in just one day—Dr. Lown, Geraldine, Ellen, Volodya, Jody, Rob, my intern, and finally Tak.

"I save the best for last," Tak said, smiling. "You don't have anything bad to tell me, do you?" David and I assured him that we didn't. We talked about the amazing new antinausea drug that doesn't make me sleepy. I've barely noticed any nausea at all from my four chemo drugs. In fact, I ate filet mignon today! This antinausea drug costs $600 a day. I told all my visitors that the insurance company is paying $600 a day for me to have the use of my mind. I'm doing my best to make it worth the money.

Bucky Fuller was right: The artist mends the universe, holds it together against the force of entropy—the tendency toward dissolution, alienation. Making a work of art, writing a clear statement of truth—these hold the universe together. Even if the painting or poem is destroyed or tucked in a drawer, even if the song is sung with no one to hear, the great fabric of the universe receives another shining stitch. Any act of love is art. Even a smile at a toll booth operator.

I walk around the floor, pushing my IV pump as fast as I can, raising a cone of power, feeling an intense rush of health welling up inside me and spilling out in an unmistakable radiance. At first, the nurses and docs look away, embarrassed. By my seventh or eighth lap they cannot help smiling. By lap thirteen or fourteen, they are laughing and calling out, "Don't mow anyone down!" "Better get out of *your* way!" I catch the eyes of my fellow patients, and a woman smiles at me from her bed. I have on my new Reeboks. I move fast and sleek. As I whizz past, one nurse comments, "Nothing wrong with that kid. What's she doing here?" The pole careens as I whirl around corners. A senior physician nods in approval, and I think: "I am helping him love his job." On lap eighteen a blond, sturdy physical therapist catches me and asks, "Would you like a bike?" She wheels a stationary cycle into my room, and after my twenty-four laps I do a solid ten-mile ride.

There are so many opportunities to love, even on the fourteenth floor of a cancer institute.

Today, I was suddenly aware of the long journey we have traveled, as a species, to get to where we are now. Millions of choices by millions of people brought me to this tall, immaculate, allopathic hospital with its strong resistance to death. As I eyed the needles and drugs, the small and big machines, all the evolutionary wonder of the place, it struck me: This is not such a bad place to be. In one sense, human history has been a series of disasters since the Indo-Europeans invaded Europe roughly 5,000 years ago, bringing with them a culture of warfare and domination. There has been so much destruction and pain. But the sharp edge of human will has carved out beauty and opportunity, too, and it has brought us to a place still teeming with potential. We can never know what might have been, never know what the world would be like if the goddess-worshipping peoples of old Europe, who lived in relative harmony with each other and with nature, had not been invaded. But at least we can be grateful for Bach, Bulgarian dance, and the Dana-Farber Cancer Institute. As I pushed my IV pole down the corridor, I felt gratitude, a remarkable sense that in some ways, I am exactly where I should be. In some ways, everything is proceeding according to plan.

This is not to be confused with the Panglossian "All's for the best in this best of all possible worlds," or its modern version, "We're all evolving to a higher consciousness and everything is guaranteed to work out." We must behold the continuous mix of triumph and disaster, and realize that while the drama unfolds, no outcomes, "good" or "bad," are guaranteed. What we do matters. This is the work.

"I have been thinking of you so much," said Ellen. "You are teaching us a lot," added Dawn. The circle dance in Rockport last night was dedicated to me, and on Sunday they will sing with me in their hearts. Love. Love everywhere, springing forward, the carpets of flowers under the burnt trees.

"You still have a very curable disease," an intern told us. "Some people have been tracked for ten or even twenty years past transplant, and they're fine. You're young, you're tough, you've got a good attitude. Some people go into transplant with the attitude, 'This is the last horrible thing I have to endure before I die.' It won't be like that for you. It'll be a gamble but it will be worth it."

Statistics. Okay, fine. The statistics aren't so great. But they aren't so great for the planet, either! Let's hear it for the golden goddess of

Exception, lovely Exception springing into the world, winging through the trees like a jeweled warbler. Exception: You are our real teacher. Welcome, 50 percent!—ruddy-faced, cheerful, muscular, a little stocky, with sleeves rolled up over your arms! Welcome, 40 percent! Slender and beautiful in light blue, a young woman with golden hair, long white arms, and a wise, if slightly sad, face. You are still much stronger than the chances for the world. Why should I be afraid of you?

June 10

My last night in the hospital was a hard one. My bed broke, and I had to move to one nearer the noisy hall. My platinum was running slowly, my nurse told me she would hang the high-dose Ara-C around 3:00 A.M. I felt nervous about its brain toxicity, and feared that by morning my grace and coordination would be gone and I would never dance again. I could not sleep, and finally asked for a sleeping pill. My arm began to ache, and I realized one of my two IV's was going bad. The nurse switched to the other catheter but it hurt and I still could not sleep. I asked the Goddess to come, and she appeared at my bedside, saying, "My daughter, you will always be able to dance." Oh, the struggle for health goes on and on; it is never clearly won or lost. Every effort, every act of love, matters. In the movie *Wings of Desire,* it is the task of the angels to witness the beauty and pain of the human spirit, to notice every gesture of love, beauty, truth, compassion—to record it and then celebrate it.

June 11

3:00 A.M.

Home. After a peaceful seven hours of sleep, I have eaten some dinner (cheese on crackers, a little tea with honey) in the still hours of this cool summer night. I am happy to lie in my own bed, surrounded by love. The only true horror possible in life: to know that others would not care if you lived or died. To know, too late, that you had not loved enough, that you had not woven enough threads, so that when you slipped away, few felt the tugs. But my news runs through a vast interconnected network, ripples and hums, and pulls forth tears, anger, and dialogues with God.

Outside my window, indigo clouds, the soft gleaming sliver of the waning moon. Now is the banishing time. The drugs are performing their magic banishing dance. The exorcism is in full swing! Sing praises to the waning moon!

June 12

Today's god is sweet and doe-eyed, a wet-faced boy in the mists, with a cherubic, impish grin. It's 5:00 A.M., dawn, and there is peace in the air after last night's storm. I write by candlelight with a cup of tea nearby as Sister Mockingbird holds court in the juniper. Today could go either way—several hours in the clinic hooked up to two pints of fresh blood. Or here, overseeing the move to a new house down the street. I honestly have no opinions as to which I prefer: no anxieties about the outcome. I'll flow with it, as I'm slowly learning to do. Yes, this is training. Winning good new habits. It does not take virtue so much as practice.

None of the struggles with constipation, cramps, diarrhea, tiredness, a mild vaginitis, are fazing me very much, this time. They are all on the surface, all just at the skin. The real fight is going on invisibly, underneath. Monday afternoon I could still hear a slight wheeze. When I asked, "What's happening in there?" Tak replied, "Hopefully it's saying 'Ouch!' and going away!" This childlike answer from the Great Lymphoma Expert appealed to me. When I asked how many centimeters it had grown, he looked right at me and said, "Several." Back to a kiwi, in no time.

"What caused the wheeze?" I asked.

"The tumor is not compressing the airway," he said, "but maybe the airway is irritated at this thing right next to it, and it's complaining."

That's it. These cells started jumping up and down, waving their arms and yelling, "Gale! *Gale!* Pay attention, Gale! Something's going on!" Which they did not do last fall. I interpret this as progress. The citizen watchdog groups in my body are now mobilized, and they call in immediately on the hotline to report anything suspicious.

How do I accept that the tumor grew back so fast, so vigorously, so quickly? Does this mean I really am peculiarly susceptible to its power? That on some basic level it is too strong for me? If the damn thing comes back again after the transplant, can I will it away through sheer stubbornness? This last thought is comforting—but it is also terrifying. I do not want to tempt the gods. I could fall into the trap of arrogance. David, here, was a wise fellow priest. "If the transplant doesn't work, you don't have to accept the medical model," he said. "Reread Bernie Siegel's book about cures of 'incurable' cancers. Remember that medicine is not an exact science. And you can pray. You can humbly, earnestly pray that the transplant will be enough. True prayer is never arrogant." Mine will not be a weak plea, "Dear God, I can't take it, please spare me," but a sincere, respectful request: "Let this be enough."

The first time, I *was* arrogant. "Licked that, no problem!" I was not humble enough before the tumor's strength. I've since learned that this journey is never "over." There is not some permanent state of "cure"—at least not for quite a while. There is no single outcome, only a succession of small outcomes, heaped and quivering one after another. I must keep paying attention. From now on, prayer comes *in advance.* I have praying to do just to get as far as the transplant—this tumor is still alive in me. I pray for time to make decisions, time to explore my fears. And I say in plain language: God and Goddess, I need your help. Let the medicines, your gifts, work within me. I need your strength. I cannot do it all alone.

Even as you discover your world-changing power, you must also learn the path of humility.

June 18

> *And so long as you haven't experienced*
> *this: to die and so to grow,*
> *you are only a troubled guest*
> *on the dark earth.*
>
> —Goethe, "The Holy Longing" (1814),
> translated by Robert Bly

I sat in the blue reclining chair of a windowless room at the cancer institute, and read the poetry that I had packed for the Grand Canyon. A few patients are sleeping, one nurse is unrolling gauze, another bringing juice. Yesterday blood started pouring out of my womb. I overflowed four pairs of underwear. I changed tampons every hour and still, endless bright red blood. The womb is letting go, all at once, and with abandon. I slept with a towel pinned around me like a diaper, and with a washcloth, too, between my legs. But dark rivulets still ran down my thighs this morning. The blood does not know how to age and clot, darken and die. There is too much youth and freshness to this blood, not enough platelets to curb it, slow it down. Poor little platelets! We came in for a platelet count and found it a mere 14.

June 19

How strange this disease, at once severe and easygoing. Except for a bit of tiredness, a small ache in my shoulder, I feel perfectly well and have walked to the beach. I received a questionnaire from the Brigham Hospital Tumor Registry. It asked only one question: "What is the current condition of your health?" The choices were "excellent," "good," "fair," and "poor." This question stumped me, so much so that I finally threw the letter away. I have a malignant tumor in my chest, so I suppose "poor" would make the most sense, yet I could not mark it. I wanted to say "excellent," or at least "good" with a p.s. "all things considered." My health *is* excellent! This is what I feel inside.

Is this denial? Am I once again underestimating the danger? Without the initial therapy, I remind myself, I would now be dead. Without the latest therapy I would be gasping for breath. Yet I am better off than a lot of the "healthy" people around me who seem, by and large, asleep. Asleep! So many people, completely unaware of their bodies and their lives. The only difference between you and me, I want to say, is that someone switched on my internal light, and now it is hot and incandescent.

The blood has slowed down to a normal flow. Tak is delighted that my platelet count "bumped up" to 81. An excellent response. It bodes well for the transplant. It means my body is open to help. The person who made these platelets and gave them voluntarily is helping me very much. Thank you, dear person. I am learning to accept gifts, humbly. Gifts of medicines, gifts of blood.

I have let so many things go in this year. I am stripped clean and bald. I have let go of my work in Russia and my trips to the desert, the wilderness, the mountains. Let go of having children, moving West. Let go of book parties, even of my book's "success." So much letting go, and still so much is left. David, family and friends, writing, poetry, ocean stars sun sky laughter music.

June 20

I have walked to the ocean and swum in the healing waters. Can I really be so ill? In the middle of the night, I felt warm. As I threw the covers off, I thought, If this is a fever, I must fight it off. I slept fitfully, and woke knowing the danger had passed.

Tonight, curled up in David's arms, a strange cough and a quick shiver of fear. Could it be growing again, already?

I'm no longer as good as a coin toss. But to hell with statistics! Fear is my guide through the dark country to real prayer and real choice. It's time to make my choice: I love David so much I am not ready to leave! (Good girl, thatta way!) Yet I seem to be missing something. What is it in me that doesn't want to hang on to life too fiercely, that is afraid of failure? Perhaps I am doing what I criticize others for: protecting myself from hope, preferring to be pessimistic and right rather than hopeful and disappointed. Oh, it is a hard lesson, my Goddess, yet I feel you are trying to teach me to face the possibility of failure—the failure to will myself into life and health. Failure is a harder demon for me than death itself. Yes, I love David. I want life. I must mobilize everything, and still accept that it may not be enough. But pray that it *will* be enough. And yet, I may end up dead rather soon, despite everything. A shiver of fear, cold and bright as moonlight, rides on a single cough, a tiny sensation of tightness in the chest.

I cannot will what will be, yet my will does matter. This is the paradox. Releasing control and yet taking on full-fledged responsibility.

June 21, Solstice

I tell my friends that the first six months of cancer was my master's degree in love and life. Now I'm in the doctoral program. I've got some intense research ahead and then I'll write my thesis. My brother said, "Well, for heaven's sake, don't go for a post-doc!" He's right. But for me the essence of this journey remains learning. Learning that will not end with the next remission or with the transplant.

June 22

I am facing death yet setting sail for the isle of rebirth. It is the day after solstice. To think about the inevitable waning of the sun, now, in high summer. Today I face a new challenge. The wheeze has definitely returned. It is slight, still, but unmistakable. It can be heard most clearly when I laugh.

David is angry at the tumor. He worries that I am not expressing anger, that I seem too calm, too convinced that there is time for exploration, when in fact the situation is very urgent. He reminded me: I can't have a transplant at the Dana-Farber if I don't get back into remission.

Anger is good, anger awakens and impassions, but anger does not sustain you over the long haul. I can't stay angry at my tumor forever. I need to go a step beyond that, into love and compassion. I must love, love, love my lymphocytes, and hold out a vision of healing for them. I cannot hate the tumor or pretend the cancer is something separate and external.

Yesterday I read about the maiming of sharks. The fins are cut off and sold for eight dollars and twelve dollars a pound at Asian markets to make soup. The sharks' bodies are mutilated and tossed overboard. I felt a connection to the four hundred-million-year-old unchanging ones of the deep, and then I got angry. I got angry at the Mendocino loggers who destroyed a precious ten-acre grove of old-growth redwoods out of spite. And I got angry at the destruction of Burma's teak forests, sold to finance a military dictatorship. But anger itself will not sustain change. Anger will burn itself out. The thin, wispy, dry kindling will not make coals, even if piled on in abundance. So it feels dangerous to get angry at my tumor. Anger is so urgent, it believes we have no time for love. I must convince myself I do have time for this deeper process.

This morning the wheeze is unmistakable. Dammit! It's growing and I have hardly a white cell in my body to stop it. An unexpected blow. Just how strong is this damn thing? My blood counts are still too shaky from my last chemo to make immediate treatment very likely. But I want to go back to the hospital. I want more platinum and other drugs, fast. Go, white blood cells! Go, marrow!

Smack! Here I am up against another demon: anxiety. I wonder, Am I doing enough? I'm not doing macrobiotics. I'm not doing beets or intravenous vitamin C. I'm not pushing myself to run two miles a day. Am I too complacent? How much is enough? This is like our race to heal the world. We work to save a little marsh, then read about destruction elsewhere. We write letters about prisoners of conscience in Vietnam. But what about all the letters that go unwritten for prisoners in Burma, Guatemala, Iraq? Guilt comes from living in a world of wounds. We could always be doing more, yet there is a paradox here, some counterforce which declares that unless what you do *feels like* enough, doing more will only backfire. The key question is: Am I doing what is right and true for me? And at the same time, can I forgive and love myself despite all I'm not doing? Just as the oak tree is fully an oak, I must be fully and completely Gale. I cannot let the false god of guilt prevent me from enjoying the sweet taste of life, from seeing the glass as half full. No, I am not "doing everything," but I am doing what feels right.

Then there's that other demon, fear of failure. What if I really go for it, but nothing works? I found the answer in Martin Buber's *I and Thou*, in a passage I underlined ten years ago: "(A) free human being encounters fate as the counter-image of his freedom. It is not his limit but his completion; freedom and fate embrace each other to form meaning; and given meaning, fate—with its eyes, hitherto severe, suddenly full of light—looks like grace itself."

We won't *encounter* our fate unless we *fully* mobilize our will. We will not know whether things could have turned out differently unless we act on our full potential, unless we choose to reach for the limit.

We must walk out to meet our fate. We must walk to the edge of the canyon, the top of the mountain, into the cold waters of the ocean. We cannot stay safe and snug in our houses, predicting the worst. If the worst is there, we must go out and find it.

The resistance in my airway, the persistence of the tumor, reminds me to go out to meet my destiny. To look into its "hitherto severe" eyes until they become full of grace.

That I cannot accomplish my healing in the exact way I intend—this reveals a mystery to me. The beauty and mystery of cosmic resistance! What has long been labeled "God's will." The unseen dance partner of our will, whose steps we can only deduce.

I spent this morning in the hospital, tired and discouraged. I pulled out this notebook and wrote for more than two hours. I do not like listening to my own labored breath.

The dictionary defines *discouragement* this way: "That which destroys or abates courage; that which lessens confidence or hope." Has my courage been abated? Or is it just being awakened for the first time? David had a vision of me, years hence, giving a speech to an audience of young women. At times the words just well up in me. But the wheeze coming back is so discouraging. I must take it as an opportunity to hunt down the courage that today slipped quietly into the forest. I must stalk it, find it, appreciate its beauty, ask it to walk by my side.

June 23

Today's god leans back on a sailboat cleaving the fresh waves. There are wispy white clouds like mare's tails and more sailboats off the beach than I have ever seen. The wheeze progresses in its steady, inimitable way, yet I am determined to sing and dance today.

I've been thinking about Mark Dubois. Mark is a river boatman who in the 1970s staved off the drowning of the majestic Stanislaus River Canyon under an encroaching reservoir. He knew the canyon better than anyone and probably loved it more, too. He fought for years to save it, but without success. So, as the canyon was filling up behind the dam, he went to a secret place at the edge of the rising water, chained himself to a rock, threw away the key, and told only a newspaper reporter where he was. "I have attached my life to the life of the canyon," he said. "If they are going to take the canyon they can take me with it." Helicopters couldn't find him but the officials believed he was out there. So they opened the dam and let the spring runoff flow through. A few years later, though, the reservoir was filled.

As I struggle against despair I think of Mark Dubois as he watched the canyon drown, knowing he had fought hard but wondering whether, if he had been a little more clever, he might have saved it. To keep hope alive when it appears we are losing. It's much easier to say than to do. Mark took seeds from the native grapevines and fruit trees of the canyon, planted them in his backyard, and nurtured them until they were strong and healthy. One day, he quietly told us, when the dam is destroyed and the canyon restored, the seeds will be replanted and the link will be unbroken.

June 25

As Martin Luther King Jr. said to the freedom marchers, if you don't know fear, you are out of touch with reality. The trick is to be afraid and still keep walking forward.

I looked at my new X ray today and saw the tumor. It is fairly large. Tak said the tumor "looked stable." A clever choice of words, meaning it is the same size it was three weeks ago when I started the treatment. We are barely holding even with it, so we have to try something else: a course of radiation to put out this brushfire.

The tumor is about to see a whole new warrior approach. A male sun, a light saber, a southern fire. The healing yellow-white beam will start just after the summer solstice, the solar peak. Once again, cosmic synchronicities!

Tomorrow I will meet a new member of the team—Peter Mauch, head of the lymphoma division of radiation therapy for all the Harvard hospitals. It is not so hard to listen to my scuba-tank breath, now that we have a plan. It is an eerie sound—a low bottle-whoosh that continues for several seconds after I finish breathing in. Tak says my entire airway is visible on the X ray, clear, unobstructed, uncompressed. Perhaps the tumor creates an irritation that makes mucus and that in turn creates the sound.

"You keep trying to . . . *hoodwink* us," Tak said, "but I'm not discouraged yet."

The radiation doc is going to have to aim carefully to avoid the spinal cord (my tumor's asymmetry is helpful here). He's the same guy who'll be doing the radiation for the transplant, so he can plan it all in advance and avoid giving me too high a dose in any one place.

My energy is good. My blood cell count is rising, too. I credit the laughter, dance, and singing. I may even hang on to much of my hair for a while! My veins will have time to recover. Still, after my blood test, I cried.

Just as I was wiping my tears, a woman came up to me in the waiting room and handed me a red rose. Tak asked if David had bought it. I said, with a smile, "Sometimes life just hands you a rose."

June 26

In the cool morning, despair and terror whisper things behind my back. I hear only snatches of words, until I get mad and turn around and surprise them: "Speak! Show your face!"

Despair whispers: The tumor is stronger than you. It is stronger than David, Tak, the medicines. It is stronger even than the Goddess. It is unstoppable. It already has taken root firmly in your body. You had one chance, and you blew it. Now it's running the show. The tumor has a death grip on your chest. You may kill off a lot of its cells but there will always be more. In time you will again feel the breath compress, hear the rattle in the chest, and know the doctors have run out of tricks.

Despair continues: Training! Ha! It may be training, but just when you have gained the knowledge, the tumor will take it all away. And people you love will think, Our prayers didn't work. Nothing we do matters at all.

June 27

Early morning. Walking the beach, alone, talking aloud.

"If the radiation doesn't work, this story may be over rather soon. How do I feel about that? It doesn't feel too good! But then, I'm not wise enough to know all the answers. If this is my hour of power, if this is my time of greatest teaching, then it is enough. I have no real complaints. I have led a candlelight ritual of hope and change within sight of the Kremlin towers. I have seen whales and penguins. I have spent the night in a volcano. Made love by the firelight. Chanted in sweat lodges. I've written books, essays, poems, and articles. I have helped to change lives, even the world. Is it greedy to want more? It doesn't feel like greed. I don't feel insistent and bossy, demanding more as if it were my entitlement. Yet I do want more. I want to stay here with David and my family and friends, I want to ride more rivers, climb more mountains, swim in more seas. What is this wanting more, if it is not greed? What is its name?"

I turned and walked in the other direction, ankle deep in the sea, toward the sun. I tried different words aloud: Is it the will to live? The will to love? Choice? Preference? Desire?

"Desire," I said, testing it. "Is its true name desire?"

The desire of the barnacles for the rock. Of the oceans for the moon. The desire of the new leaf for the sun. It is not exactly love, this energy, this push, this straining and reaching for more. It is desire. It is not the "will to live." Merely living is not enough to motivate us. Getting up and eating and doing tasks and going to sleep—this doesn't pull me forward. It's rather limp. But desire! And I have desires, I have deep desires, and I must live in order to fulfill them.

The desire of the cormorants for the warm winter lagoons. The desire of lichens embracing granite with embroidered passion. The desire of the forest that springs from the burned valley. This deep desire we have for one another's bodies.

Greed is anxious and incomplete, an inner emptiness crying to be filled, but the cries go unanswered. Greed knows no limits.

Desire appreciates all it already has, loves itself, and yet reaches joyfully for more. Desire understands limits and is willing to release, to let chicks fly from the nest, leaves fall from branches, love affairs end. The barnacle lets go.

Always, the paradox of desire and release. When yogis speak of the end of desire, what they really mean is the end of greed and grasping, for they desire Brahma greatly.

Desire sings praises even as it desires!

We sing praises even as we desire!

The desire of electrons for protons, of positive charges for negative. The electric desire of gamma rays, of radiation beams! May that desire work magic in my body and meld with my own deep desires, that I've just begun to name and own.

Did it really take cancer to make me into a writer? I sigh as I ask the question, knowing the answer could be "yes." To be an artist, a visionary, takes a focused training in today's world of so many distractions. For me, cancer is this training. But I must have time to use it.

"Okay, my Goddess, are you listening? I promise—no, I swear by the sacred waters of the mother ocean! Let the radiation work. Let the transplant work. Give me more time and I'll write my fingers down to the bone. I can love David from the blue road of spirit, I can help the planet from the blue road of spirit, but dammit, I can't write if I'm dead!"

The demons come, curiously, in the morning. I whirl around, sick of the whispering, and try to see their faces before they hide again. This morning, it was terror. Terror in the gut, heavy, paralyzing. With fear you are still free, you can still move, you can walk forward. Terror paralyzes. It takes away the breath, it blanks out desire, motivation. It says, "You're fooling yourself to think you can escape this fate. One by one your fine 'explanations' and positive interpretations and faith and confidence will wither away. They will all prove hollow and meaningless."

I look terror, the sister of despair, in the face. I curl up in bed and surrender to great racking sobs of misery. "Lord, why me? What the hell is going on? This is not what I had in mind. Did I pick up the wrong script last week?"

I know to be initiated as a shaman you must go through a real test—the shaking of confidence and faith to the roots. But I have a bad feeling about all this. I'm not confident in the radiation, in my body, in the transplant. This tumor has succeeded in terrifying me with its persistence. What is next?

I am writing for my life, and oh, it is not as easy as it sounds. You can't just snap your fingers and blithely announce, "I want to live!" and have a sudden flood of deep inner resources automatically surge through your being. I have to work. I have to unlock the deep desires, the desire of my heart to keep beating, of my brain to keep on flashing and creating, of rivers of blood and lymph to keep on flowing. The demons, the grinning ugly gremlins of despair scuttle out of reach when I whirl around to face them—yet they hold some of the keys.

"So you're here, you miserable monsters. We have much to discuss! You shrink away on this bright morning, but I know you'll be back! I have grabbed one key already. One tiny, golden key that unlocks desire and opens me to my natural fullness. Despair says, 'You can't change anything!' But I banish it and say, 'I am a daughter of the four winds, a child of moon and rain and sun. I am sister to the whale, the osprey, and the juniper. I belong here. The desires of my kin are my desires. I am a seed that desires to root, to grow, and to blossom.' "

June 29

She strips to the waist. The attendants place her on the table. They pull her arms up so her chest is exposed, defenseless. They wheel her into the center of the room. A round light expands and contracts, clicking on and off as they adjust the lens above her. They identify the tumor on a screen and carefully mark its boundaries. They survey her landscape. They work with precision. They come toward her with their pens. In the mirror of the lens, she sees the blue and orange dots they've marked on her breasts, her chest, her shoulders, her neck. They check again. She hears numbers—15 and 22. The room darkens, the attendants leave, the lights flash. Her arms begin to ache. Her back begins to ache. Suddenly she feels a piercing pain in the shoulder, in the belly, in the face near the left eyebrow. Her breath comes faster, she nearly faints. There is no sound from the three helpers. She wiggles her toes. She thinks, The old pain has returned! The technicians come in. She is permitted to lower her arms. Her hands are numb. She opens and closes them. They fold a wire across her breast. With a metal caliper they measure her chest again and again, and take snapshots with a flash camera. They leave and return with a needle and some blue dye. She is going to be tattooed. She will receive ten tiny sacred marks of initiation, where the radiation will come in. She counts as the needle pricks the skin. She feels the tiny hot pain, the irrevocability, and she almost smiles. The attendant washes her, and tells her it is done.

Fear is not the only demon. There is also panic, a closed-in feeling, a paralyzing presence. A deer frozen in the headlights.

Panic says, "I have so much to do but no time to do it!" I thought I had several more months before my bone marrow transplant—now they are talking about having me go in very soon. Everything is accelerating and the new pace is dizzying.

This is another teaching. Our assumptions about time are illusory. We think we have time to patch up a relationship, then the person breaks off contact. We think we have time to write a novel, then suddenly we are uninspired. We believe we have time to preserve the rain forests, figure out a solution to nuclear waste. Yet time is running out and we have, in fact, only the present moment. The river keeps picking up speed. The transplant will be very soon, before the leaves begin to turn. So I call a moratorium, a four-day retreat. I feel revelations stacked up inside me, and I will collapse if I cannot pull them out and write them down.

Hair comes out in three-quarter-inch-long wisps, on the pillow, the towel, the shoulders of my white shirt. I am shedding a second time. I am ripening and aging like a fruit. I finger the pale stiff fuzz left on my head. It is no longer a thick doglike coat that asks to be stroked and petted. I look in the mirror and think, I could still go out in public. My eyebrows are unchanged. I look better with eyebrows and am grateful for them. I pull a clutch of hair from my head, and say, "I am the Woman Who Lost Her Hair Three Times." In another language, a syllabic language, close-rooted to the earth, this could be a beautiful name. Angakuapetalepala, for example. An-ga-kua-pe-ta-le-pa-la. The Woman Who Lost Her Hair Three Times. Will it grow back during the radiation, a soft pale underfuzz like grass under the trees?

June 30

Cool steady rain outside, wonderful to awaken to. A little dancing this morning, a breakfast of rice and eggs. The breath makes strange whimpery, gurgly sounds. I cough if I breathe deep. My friend Gail laughed when I told her my breathing is so shallow that I don't have time to recite Thich Nhat Hanh's meditation verse, "Breathing in, I feel like a flower. Breathing out, I feel fresh." The best I can do is, "Flower—fresh—flower—fresh." I long to fill my lungs with a great, clean sweep of air, to feel that old expansiveness, but I must learn to be more modest.

On the beach, I drew in the sand the splayed-out, vulnerable DNA of my tumor cells, with gamma rays landing on them like little hot meteorites. During those two minutes of treatment, I must tell the tumor cells to *go*, while advising my healthy cells to just hang tight. "Right," said David. "Taunt the tumor cells, 'Come out of your foxholes!' Tell the others, 'Duck!' " Still, some healthy cells will have to be sacrificed. I love the faithful cells in my skin, breasts, throat, trachea, and spinal cord. Some of these will die for me in the next few weeks. I remind myself I do this out of love.

The tumor has no soul. It is like a golem, a soulless creature that can possess people and command their lives. Some people are solid tumor; the golem is fully in command. To fight it, we have the chemotherapy of hard love, the piercing radiation of God's eye. All of us have some cancer, some golem, even if we are healthy. None of us can be overconfident. With vigilance, prayer, and attention, we must nurture our spirit every day. Choosing to act out of love. This is preventive medicine.

No one is beyond the reach of healing and compassion. In the elevator lobby of the parking lot, there is a quote from Dr. Sidney Farber: "There is no such thing as a hopeless case." This is true for cancer of the soul, as well. "Amazing grace, how sweet the sound, that saved a wretch like me . . ." Those words were written by the former captain of a slave ship.

David remarked, "This all sounds very Christian." I find much good in Christianity. But Christianity has a limited understanding of death. It says we only have one chance, then we fall this way or that for all eternity: "You make it or you fail." Christianity says little about the great round of death and rebirth; it shuts its eyes to the cyclical nature of the universe, the whirling spiral dance.

Simple Christianity is preached by millions. But we must allow for the shimmering spectrum in between yes and no, once and forever. I understand the pressures to simplify, to speak plainly. Yet Christ often spoke of mystery and paradox. One wonders how much was censored, how many subtle teachings the Church sacrificed and replaced with dogma. Richard Bach alludes to this in his novel, *One*: Did Christ ever wonder if others would take his mandate to teach too far?

On the hospital admission form was the question, "Is religion important to you?" The choices were "yes" and "no." It was easy to mark "yes," but the next question was tougher. "What kind?" There was about an inch-long line for this. They wanted a label, an ID tag, a sticker for the file folder. Some possibilities passed through my mind. Earth-based spirituality? Goddess religion? Paganism? These seemed so incomplete. Finally inspiration came, and I wrote, with great satisfaction, "private." My religion is very important to me, and it is private. It is the power that acts through me. It is inseparable from who I am. It is, in many ways, tremendously public, since it informs my every action in the world—but it is private in the sense of "personal," "mine."

The other fabulous thing on this admission form, along with queries about allergies, past medical conditions, current medications, and so on, was: "How has your illness affected your perceptions of yourself?" They provided exactly half a line—about three inches—for an answer. I was once again stumped. "You give this much space to answer this!" I wrote, scrunching in the words. "If you really want to know, come and talk to me!"

Wednesday night we went to see a comedy at the Gloucester Stage Company. The acting was earnest, but the script was mediocre. I was supposed to laugh, and couldn't, so instead I got a stomachache. The pessimism that tried to pass for humor made my gut tighten and ache. It was a kind of cynical self-loathing.

I think there is a feeling ever since the Holocaust and the invention of atomic bombs, that our species is fundamentally flawed and not worth saving. The self-hater perches on our shoulder, loud and insistent. We do not yet love ourselves enough to heal ourselves. We must learn to appreciate our own sparkle and beauty. If we are going to save ourselves and our planet, we are going to do it out of deep love for ourselves, for all the brilliance, humor, and compassion of which we are capable.

This is where art and culture come in. These are mirrors of our humanity. They can help us recognize our common yearnings and desires. We must look in these mirrors and rekindle our self-love. Marvel at ourselves—our poets and storytellers, weavers and painters, musicians and dancers, potters and playwrights, sculptors and novelists, wood carvers and choreographers, ice-skaters and dressmakers, chefs and trapeze artists.

How can we expect to love humanity if we do nothing but stare at images of horror? Our television screens show murder, robbery, and child abuse, people burned to death and floods in Bangladesh. This feeds our despair. I'm not talking about turning away from evil or cruelty. We must face these dark shadows. But in the media we encounter only the surface of suffering. We indulge ourselves in horror, voyeuristically, getting a thrill from swooping close. We titillate ourselves and say, "We are facing facts" when we are really doing nothing. We overexpose ourselves and go numb.

"Protect yourselves," urged Thich Nhat Hanh at a meditation workshop we attended. "Newspapers, magazines, and television programs show only what is wrong. Within ourselves are the seeds of despair and the seeds of peace. We must choose to water the seeds of peace."

About half of the patients with my type of lymphoma are cured by bone marrow transplants. Tak says the goal is to have about 1,000 cancer cells remaining after the transplant. The hope is that the body can take care of these cells on its own. The immune system, the body's own self-healing ability, is the mystery ingredient.

The cancer began, perhaps, with one cell that became ten, that became a hundred, that become a thousand, that became ten thousand, that became a million, that became a billion. If my body let this happen once, why not again? Just because slavery existed for centuries didn't mean it could not be abolished. War is not inevitable and neither is my illness. We have to train ourselves to see our own aliveness. If we start believing we are already dead, or too far gone to save, we will be right.

Four women called to give me their love, women who have become wise through suffering. I hold them around me, see their loving, kind faces: Ellen, Joan, Gail, Geraldine. Then I begin to remember others who have reached out to me: Joanna, Sharon, Amy, Jeanne, and Cynthia. Women I love enter the room—Galina, Alyona, Robin, Susan, Zhenya, and my mother. Margaret, Martha, Sara, Jennifer, Melissa, Dawn, Julie, Laurel. I feel absolutely safe, here in their arms. Something opens in me as I allow myself to receive their love. They are my sister-priestesses, the ones with the power to work magic.

Hunger draws the whale to the herring, but it is desire that pulls the whale out of the sea in one gigantic leap. Hunger spurs us to "get by," but desire compels us to make beauty, to play. Desire is the acrobatics of seagulls and dolphins, the jeweled throat on the hummingbird. Charles Darwin thought survival of the fittest explained it. H. C. Watson knew it didn't. He called this extra flash and swirl a divine gift, an implant from God. The life force isn't pitted endlessly against the death force, it goes somewhere. The circle rises as it spirals. The extra flick takes effort, yet it is always a possibility. To praise, to make beauty, to join in the dance.

July 1

This morning our meditation was made challenging by a loud chainsaw next door. We stuck with it and toward the end I began breathing easier and deeper. It felt so good to let my chest expand, to feel the air moving up and down my spine! Last summer I was tired and racked with mysterious pain. And yet here I am, feeling pretty good, able to control the pain, enjoying going to the beach every day. Who says this tumor is stronger than I am? We have some uneasy truce, just now.

Still, Gail warned me about the warrior who believes so strongly in her ability to create her own reality that she stomps around in places that are too dangerous. She gets in trouble with her confidence: "I can do anything! I can do it all myself!" She forgets to pray. She does not open to receive. This headstrong, willful, very effective woman of action needs help more than ever. If only I can become humble and soft enough to take it in.

The Fear Demon is back and it is nasty. It may be a guide to the hidden treasures of the mountain, but he says really awful things. "This isn't the last time you will feel tightness in your chest. You pretend you are safe, but it will come again."

Then Arrogance speaks. She has a fierce, hard beauty. I am attracted to her, even though I know she could lead me to my death. "Gale, don't worry. You are strong and powerful. You can fight off anything."

It takes all my strength to turn away from her—I don't have enough to hurl her away—but I do say, "You would lure me into stepping beyond my power. I cannot fight these forces alone. If I am too proud to accept help, if I am too proud to ask the Goddess, 'Let this be enough,' then I am tempting death. And I may lose."

Then I whirl around, trying to get a glimpse of the most elusive, silent, terrifying demon of all. At first I want to name it death, but this is not right. It is something closer to fear of death. Oh, how I resist looking at it! I am terrified to imagine letting down my guard, to stop believing "I will live!" even for an instant. To imagine death even for a moment is to let it slip through my life-force shields, give it an entry, allow it a dangerous grip on my spirit. Yet I know the time has come to face it. Dear Goddess, I ask for strength and protection while it speaks. I need faith that I can tolerate these words, that if despair enters me I can cast it out again.

The demon says: "You think this is initiation but you are wrong. You think that on the other side of this will be life and power, but you are wrong. You are on a short path and your time is near. There will be futile treatments, dashed hopes, fresh disappointments. You will never complete this book. You will never raft the Canyon or return to Russia. You will leave so many people behind. You will leave this body you love so much. I know this is difficult for you to grasp on a warm summer day when you are barefoot and tan and only the fast rise and fall of your chest gives you away. Look at me, my daughter. I am the White Woman of Death, and you are in more danger than it seems.

"You thought you would have to wrest a key from me, but I will give it to you freely. My realms are glorious for those who are ready to enter. You can embrace the adventure of death with the same zest that you embrace all of life's adventures. People meet me with various degrees of courage and enthusiasm. Some are brave enough to be fully conscious at their transformation; they are the angels, the 'helpers from the other side,' the bodiless beings of swirling light.

"This is my realm. Of course, you are attracted by its beauties. This will serve you well. But now you must try to imagine yourself leaving your body behind, for good—no going back. No meeting again of your loved ones with a body to touch them. No body to soak up the sun, to hear the crows and the wind in the trees. Do not give this life up lightly, my daughter, or underestimate how great and precious it is. There are beings in my realm who every day decide to give up their wisdom in order to take form and be born again. Stop for a moment and try to imagine you have only one year left. My words barely register, you are so alive in your body, so accustomed to savoring the world. You feel altogether too healthy now. But this is the evil trick of your cancer: It leaves you an illusion of strength and normality, while under the skin something is very wrong. Try to imagine that you have only one more year. What feelings well up in you? It is so hard for you, I know, but keep trying."

A goldfinch drops spectacularly from the edge of the cliff, falling for a few heart-stopping seconds until his black wings unfold in the nick of time.

When I am taken aback by someone's generosity, I sometimes wonder, when the tables are turned, will I reach out with love this great? It is worth pondering. To love me is a risk. The people steady in their love are risking disappointment, and riding on the strong shoulders of hope.

Dr. Caplan amazed me last Thursday. David told him my tumor didn't respond adequately to the new chemo. "Bugger," said Caplan. "I'm getting pissed." When I found him in the hallway staring at one of his nuclear scan monitors, he opened his arms to hug me. My first doctor-hug at the Farber—or anywhere, for that matter. It came at a very good time. "Have a—decent—weekend," he said with a charming grimace as we left. "Love you both." I was so moved by this. This man might have to watch me die, yet he took the risk to say, "I love you."

July 2

Today I will lie down willingly and expose my defenseless chest to the awesome light saber of God. This is Dante's leap through the flames. It is a test of faith, of my willingness to trust and to receive. This healing saber cuts into my flesh with unimaginable power. Fierce packets of intense sunlight, flaming meteors from the depths of space. I am ready to take them in, yes, ready to receive!

July 3

The radiation treatment at the Brigham Hospital was both somber and ridiculous. I was identified as a "new start on Machine 6." Already I missed the cozy family feeling of the Dana-Farber. My nurse was nice enough; she showed me little maps and diagrams plotting my field, and two hideous Polaroid snapshots of me on the planning table. I looked like a Hiroshima victim! The purpose of my talk with her eluded me. I think she was trying to address any anxieties I might have, but the questions I had were ones she could not answer. The technicians were matter-of-fact, but there is no getting around it: Stripping to the waist is undignified without a sacred context, and that was hard for me to generate. The table is hard, the lighting harsh, and the machine very big. You are not supposed to feel the radiation but I felt it: a sudden tingling, a deep ripple, a little warmth. It was as if someone had dropped a stone from a great distance into a pool of water. It was over in an instant. Talk about a test of faith. To believe *this* could make any difference. All these people, all these rooms, all these machines—nothing but a magic show! Sheer voodoo!

I suppose that when I begin to notice some side effects it will be easier to believe this is a truly powerful and effective tool. Boiling water in one minute in the microwave always seemed odd to me, too. God and the Goddess never show their faces too obviously. The test of faith is blind and sensationless, beyond an occasional moment of tingling, warmth, and light. Just enough of a hint to keep me going.

David and I went to the medical library. I learned that there are battles over classifying non-Hodgkin's lymphoma that make botanical controversies pale by comparison. The tumor cells don't look so different from normal cells, but as a community they seem to have lost all sense of structure and purpose. They are disorganized, unaware of their neighbor's existence, oblivious to their aggregate meaning. They spread out across the slide in one uniform slosh. The healthy lymph nodes have a neat symmetry, a sense of things being in their place. They have a germinal center and an outer mantle. But the tumor has no sense of place. The cells are literally out of touch with their surroundings. They replicate themselves blindly, with no memory that there ever was a stream here, a forest here, a meadow there. It is simply one mass subdivision, each unit identical to the next. The pattern has been lost.

When viewed separately, the tumor cells are only slightly awry. In isolation these cells are antisocial but not really dangerous. It occurs to me that an isolated bigot is not dangerous, but when bigots reach a critical mass, band together, and form the KKK, then society has a problem. You cannot easily pick the bigot out of the crowd at the supermarket, in an elevator, on a sidewalk passing by. "But he seems so normal!" people say. The small but fundamental thing gone awry is hidden, apparent only to the trained eye.

As we looked through the books, David told me to ignore an entry under a picture called "Lymphoma, Diffuse, Large Cell." Of course, I read it: "This term refers to a large and heterogeneous group of tumors, all with a generally poor prognosis." (To hell with outdated prognostications!) I also learned that my tumor is probably white or pinkish white, and rather soft and squishy. It's called a "liquid tumor." David suggested a comparison to the white flesh of a raw fish—something without a lot of texture, but with some solidity. The scar of my first tumor is gray and underneath there's soft pinkish-white stuff extruding from the hard gray ball. It's all just hanging there like a rotten potato between the top of my lungs and my heart. Where's the compost pile?

July 4

No treatment today; the radiation department is closed for the holiday. "Tumor cells don't grow on the Fourth of July," David explained.

I woke up this morning with a thought in my head: I am afraid I will let everyone down. My fear is that everyone around me will succumb to despair if I don't make it. If I do, it will be an inspiration, a testament to empowerment and hope. The hard thing is to remind myself that this is not some kind of cosmic court in which the question of which is stronger—hope or despair—will be settled for all time. If I pull it off I'll take much of the credit, but if I don't I won't take the blame.

My white blood cell count has soared to 5.1, a number worth bragging about. I raised the number of neutrophils, the main variety of white cells, from 84 to 3,000 in eight days! How well I remember the taciturn radiation doc drawling that ideally he'd like to see my white count up to 3.5 or 4.0 by the time treatments began, but that was hardly to be hoped for, since my counts were "frail." "I'll work on it," I'd said to him. When David got my results, we slapped our hands together in a high five. Nothing frail about those numbers twenty-eight days after a massive chemo dose! I have been eating fresh food, taking vitamins, walking in the fresh air. I have been held and soothed by David. And I have been lovingly encouraging my bones and blood to recover.

This morning I called Mom and asked her about my grandmother Edna, whom I thought could be a source of strength for me.

"How long was it between her diagnosis and her death?"

"Eight years," says Mom.

Eight years! I almost dropped the phone. She survived eight years after surgery for a massive ovarian tumor? Even today that would be considered extraordinary. My grandmother was an "exceptional cancer patient" long before the term had been invented, back when Bernie Siegel was a teenager. She had no support groups, no visualizations, she fought this thing off with her own will. I was astonished. I'd assumed she'd died a few months or perhaps a year after diagnosis. She was, instead, a miracle case.

Mom told me that my grandmother knew she had a mass in her belly for a year but was too scared to tell anyone. Finally she got too sick to hide it. She went to a doctor and they removed a malignant tumor the size of a football. That was 1948. She had eight years in remission, and when she got sick again she was treated with experimental radiation. She willed herself to live until her daughter's wedding, then went home and died in July 1956: thirty-five years ago almost to the day. No wonder she keeps appearing in my thoughts, gently telling me, "I am here to help, dear granddaughter."

I could not be more pleased if I'd suddenly discovered a great poet in my ancestry. My grandmother, an extraordinary cancer survivor. And all this time, I never knew.

July 5

You don't dedicate yourself to the Goddess just once in a lifetime. You must bathe in her waters, leap through her fire, over and over again. It is a cyclical dance, not a one-time crossing of the threshold. To live every day in the light of paradox is different from hanging your hopes on a single moment of enlightenment.

So I continue to walk on the edge of sun and shadow, in the holy swift light of change. Yesterday I imagined where our rafting expedition would be right now: deep in the walls of the Grand Canyon, with the sun, the sound of the river, the canyon wrens, the cool sand, and damp green mosses. Hot smooth rock under feet, the thrill of white water, the calm mirrors of the river. *Time and the River Flowing*, as the book title goes. River time, earth time, sun time. I felt a fierce longing to be there, and also an acceptance that I never will. What is this curious paradox of desire and acceptance, the edge of sun and shadow? I am trying to do two things which seem utterly contradictory. I am trying to hang on to life, and at the same time an inner voice is saying, "You must let it go. Let go of the cliff and fall."

Months ago, at a cancer support group we were asked to visualize leaving the Earth and moving into the void of space. I resisted, fought like a wildcat. "I don't want to leave, thank you very much. I don't need to go into space to find healing light." This rebellious "no!" was appropriate and powerful. But now I need to make that journey. To make a real choice to stay I must sincerely consider the alternatives. It is so hard to imagine leaving my body. Yet I suspect that this is precisely what I must do. Lay down my sword and shield, enter the holy temple, put my life on the altar, and say, "I am a servant of the mysteries. For you, I give up all my possessions, even my life."

> *Still, the profound change*
> *has come upon them: rooted, they*
> *grip down and begin to awaken.*
>
> —William Carlos Williams, "Spring and All"

Will I be one of the first poets to have a bone marrow transplant? There is such poetry in it, even from afar. They will draw from me the very essence of my body, the marrow, and kill off the rest. My body will quite literally be a shell, unable to survive on its own, perilously close to death. My body's essence then will be put back in a ceremony of rebirth. Paul Tsongas—another of Tak's patients—had the same kind of transplant, and the same thought: My life is compressed to a test tube in the doctor's hands—for God's sake, please don't drop it! That precious stuff is frozen, yes, kept in a refrigerator, then thawed, and sent back into the body through a vein. Through a vein back to the bones. The new life returning after a journey out of the body. For days, I'll lie split and open, neither alive nor dead but something of both; raw in the balance, fierce, meek, helpless, tense with determination.

July 6

On the phone to Ellen, I sound like the monster from the deep. "No," says David, "like Darth Vader in his mask." My chest burbles and squeaks when I lie down as the soft squishy tumor splays out. I woke up with some worries—that this two-week wait for radiation therapy was very dangerous, that in the meantime it might have spread to other sites, or to my marrow. I'm completely unprotected in those areas, wholly on my own. And I miss, I really miss, my old serene confidence, and wish at times I had it back.

Joanna Macy writes in *Despair Work* about confronting her own despair for the world bristling with nuclear missiles: "In the weeks and months that followed I carried these questions inside me like a bomb in my chest."

Carl Jung says it again. "There is no birth of consciousness without pain."

How shall I begin my song
in the blue night that is settling?
In the great night my heart will go out,
toward me the darkness comes rattling
In the great night my heart will go out.

—Papago medicine woman chant

It may be dangerous for me to think beyond the transplant and imagine it not working. But my unconscious *does* imagine it. Could I live with cancer after the transplant? Maybe I could go on long enough to finish some of the writing, get to the canyon, swim with the dolphins once.

I told David that I am afraid I will let everyone down. That I worry, should I die, that people who prayed for me will perceive this as their failure, or God's failure, and will think "nothing we do or think matters."

"That won't be true for me," he said quietly.

July 8

On the way home from the treatment this morning we grabbed some food and headed west to Walden Pond. The clouds parted and we had a glorious swim, then we went folk dancing at the Scout House. I danced without stopping. My heart was pounding but I was soon too caught up in the dance to notice it. Both David and I wondered if this might be a subtle turning point. Earlier today I was not able to produce a respectable wheeze for the resident. But I did hear it swimming, and though I could sing "Amazing Grace" pretty well on the way home, I did still have to breathe harder than usual. I don't want to make any pronouncements but, oh, I am officially ready to get better! I felt so radiant during the dance that I told my old dance partner from Kentucky, "I had cancer, but I'm a lot better now."

I have had 720 radiation units so far, out of the 4,000 planned. The resident couldn't explain why radiation works. To really know how cells are killed, David pointed out, you have to know why cells live in the first place, and that is still a mystery. All we know is that radiation seems to interfere with cell replication and damage the DNA. Tumor cells are too busy replicating to repair themselves. Some are "programmed" by the radiation to die later, others just die right away.

My radiation therapy machine is a cyclotron, a circular accelerator of electrons which bombard nuclei of other atoms and boost them to higher states. These nuclei emit gamma rays, which are some of the most powerful forces in the universe. This is hot stuff. And it must work for me. It *must.*

Driving back from a friend's house today I remembered that I am very ill. For a short time I had forgotten. These moments of distraction are rare indeed.

Every night for the last five nights, I have had the cancer in my dreams. This is new. A sign perhaps that I am more deeply aware of what is going on in my body. I wait for some sign of improvement in the wheeze.

The weather remains oppressively humid, cloudy, stagnant, but my garden is flourishing, the tomatoes properly staked, and I seem to be ahead of the cabbage worms for the moment. David cheerfully provides me with one gourmet meal after another. We are waiting, waiting for the radiation to do its silent work.

July 9

A day of sunshine, dry winds, blue sky. Though I awoke with the rumbling in my lungs and a lot of coughing, the wheeze seems better. David is thrilled. I lag behind him in emotional reactions; he gets both worried and relieved before I do, so maybe I'll be feeling better soon. Some tangible progress is being made after only four radiation treatments. We'll really whack the thing this week. I'm going to keep praying and paying close attention. The pressure has lifted just a little now.

What would I say to people who have cancer, who are on the edge of despair and hope?

Never let anyone else tell you the meaning of your illness. To each of us, cancer says different things. There is no standard message, "You work too hard" or "You didn't work hard enough;" "You give yourself too much to others" or "You are too focused on yourself." These things and a hundred others may be true, but remember, for some, cancer is also a random event with no "cause." Well-meaning people may try to "interpret" your cancer for you. Perhaps what they say will be helpful, but they are speaking mostly about themselves. No one can really tell you what your cancer means; only you can give it meaning.

Susan Sontag insists that there is no meaning to cancer. "It's just a disease," she says. Others, like me, create elaborate symbols to support our healing and hope. Whatever your response, no one should ever tell you not to feel what you are feeling. If you are hurt, angry, despairing, or miserable, the last thing anyone should say is "Don't be sad. Cheer up. Think positive." If people do, gently tell them this is not helpful. If they persist, just walk away. But don't, for God's sake, put up with it. Your friends can hug you and support you, but they can't tell you what to think. Remember, your feelings, including your awful ones, are very real. If you accept them they can be your resources and your helpers. To repress feeling is always dangerous—it feeds the little fear and depression gremlins and turns them into monsters. But sunshine and attention stunt their growth.

Cancer brings opportunities for change and improvement and growth. It offers a unique challenge to each of us. It may have to do with your relationships, with your spiritual path, with finding or enhancing your true work. Ask yourself questions and listen hard for answers. They may be thunderously loud or the faintest of whispers. You may receive them with ecstatic joy—or with terror. But discovering and creating this meaning, exploring it, is your most powerful tool for getting well. Use your ingenuity to make the best of it. There are no guarantees—but perhaps that extra resolve, "Okay, you can go now. I understand your message," can make the crucial difference.

There is a misunderstanding about healing. If you mobilize your inner resources and it doesn't work, you are *not* to blame. It's not that you were too weak, or you didn't "do it right." Some cancers are simply too strong even for the most powerful of wills. Some of us will die because it is our time to die, no matter how bravely we dance out to meet our fate, how persistently we choose life. No one should ever be blamed for losing the battle. But we should definitely get credit for winning it. God, family and friends, medicines, and our own choices can tilt the balance and pull it off.

No one, including your doctor, knows your fate. I think not even God knows. That's the reason to mobilize hope and choice, to call on the power of love and life. True, it won't work in every case. But would you spurn a medicine just because it only works 20 percent of the time? Especially when taking the medicine will make you healthier and happier, when the quality of the days you have left will be so much better? The only "side effect" of hope is guilt, and that can be counteracted. Remember not to take the blame, that some cancers—and some destinies—are very strong. If you turn out to have one of these, it is still worth it to push for full healing. For your life will be richer and more beautifully lived, right to the end. How blessed to own your life, to draw power from boundless wells, to know you helped swing the balance in your favor for one timeless moment.

A second misunderstanding about healing is that we must have only positive thoughts: If I allow myself, even for a moment, to think something negative, then I will give these thoughts energy and help make them happen. This is a misunderstanding of the principles of manifestation. It is true that holding an image in our mind's eye, repeating it, affirming it, and visualizing it will help bring it out into the world. But *expressing* fears is not the same as *affirming* them. To say "I am afraid the tumor is too strong for me" is not the same as repeating "The tumor *is* too strong and I will die." Expression strips fear of its power. Repression enhances it.

Dragging those scrawny-necked little fears out into the light of day also allows you to talk back to them. In whispers, in shadows, they seem huge and unconquerable. In the light, they turn out to be manageable—sometimes even absurd. *Let the fears speak. They will not harm you.* You can answer them and put them in their place. *You* are running the show. If you remember this, your fears can become guides to the deep resources of the unconscious. Some people simply say, "I *will* get well. I *won't* think of the alternative." This is their way of holding on to a vision of health and it must be respected. Bashing through their denial could actually kill them. If you are serenely confident, if you hear no whispers or see no shadows there is no reason to go digging around for them. Some people just aren't afraid. But many are. And it is a way of gaining power to face those fears. For awhile the only genuine response to the fears I could muster was: "Maybe you're right. But maybe not." But even this feeble answer gave me power. I clung to this "maybe" for a long time before I could come up with something stronger.

Over time we shift from the victim's question "Why did this happen to me?" to "Now that this is happening, how can I make the best of it?" We can say, "This is part of God's plan," because we are also helping to make that plan. It's our plan, too. We can weave beauty and meaning from this hard dark stuff. It is not easy but when we succeed, what a contribution! At every instant, we ourselves are weaving a new piece of the tapestry.

Rabbi Kushner's book, *When Bad Things Happen to Good People*, has some helpful pointers on moving out of the victim stance. But his attempt to explain the place of chaos and evil in the universe isn't very satisfying to me. Either God is still creating the world, he says, and eventually there will be less chaos and evil, or God finished the job long ago and made an imperfect world which "we will simply have to learn to live with." But it seems to me there are more possibilities! Maybe we are cocreating the world as partners with God, moving it toward more harmony and beauty. If not counteracted, entropy would rule. But there is something going against it, weaving the threads, holding it together. Each day *we* weave some of those threads, and it is a never-ending process.

Kushner says successful prayer does not ask for outcome (someone's recovery, good grades, etc.), but courage, strength, and the inner resources to help us do what we need to. In his view, other people's prayers help us because we don't feel so alone, but they don't directly heal. He imagines a world unaffected by consciousness or intention, but I think there is more going on than he makes out. Sometimes "prayer at a distance" can help—even if we never learn about it. If the world is a swirl of currents of energies, then such things can happen. I think there is much magic in the world. In a famous study, nuns prayed for a group of cardiac patients. They healed faster than the control group even though they had no idea what was happening! Sometimes prayer doesn't work this way. But sometimes it does—why not give it a chance?

July 10

I use this time of night, just before going to bed, to write in my journal by candlelight. David is curled on his side on the futon, as innocent in his sleep as a child, and I feel such tenderness toward him.

I have had six radiation treatments and there are reasons to think they are working. The wheeze is improved. But I still have many questions. Will we shrink the tumor down enough? Will it stay down long enough for me to get the transplant?

I continue to pray each time I lie flat on the table, raise my arms overhead, and bare my chest to the healing gamma rays. . . .

July 11

I've been using the Native American Animal Cards. The card I drew this morning was Buffalo, the animal of prayer and abundance. I have been thinking a lot about prayer. Do we have guardian angels watching over us? I believe we do. But then why do we still get hurt? Do our angels slip up or stop paying attention at crucial moments? No, I rather think it's a matter of balance. There are some things angels and God can influence, and some things that resist their best efforts.

God cannot heal us alone; he needs us as full and willing partners, pulling our own weight. As long as I know I am doing this, genuinely, I can relax and say, "The rest is up to you." This is really what I mean when I say, "My life is in your hands." I mean that I am doing what I can, but know I cannot do anything without the support of all that is sacred and loving. Alone and disconnected, I am small and weak. Loved and noticed, I am large and strong and capable of miraculous things. The guardian angels are there, but they can't help if we ignore them.

Prayer is a call to partnership, a conscious placing of our spirits and intentions in alignment with the creative spirit. This call to partnership is always noticed. It affects the whole. It can help tilt the balance, draw forth hidden resources. So prayer—humble, undemanding, simple prayer—is always worth it.

Prayer also means giving thanks for gifts received. Today I woke with only the faintest of vibrations in my chest. I haven't coughed yet and my wheeze can only be heard by David's sensitive ears. Yet how easy it is to take good news as if this is what I am entitled to. I remind myself, this morning, to give thanks—to take nothing, including the radiation's apparent efficacy, for granted. I give thanks for my clean breath, my loosening lungs, my quiet inhalations. We are over the first tiny hurdle. I am grateful to God and the Goddess for bringing me this far.

Yesterday I felt the beginnings of a curious new fear—once the tumor is gone, I will have to live with the anxiety of it coming back. A return of the wheeze would probably signal my death. This is my new nightmare. On the other hand, a few years ago, the doctors would have given up on me already. "You have an incurable disease," they would have said, "relapsed B-cell non-Hodgkin's lymphoma." But I have a second chance—the transplant. Twenty, even ten years ago, people like me would have sung hosannas just to be given such an opportunity. Rather than focus on the transplant not working, I think for a moment about the odds of it actually working. I should have been dead long ago, so every day is a gift. Each week, each month of further life is an abundance. Morning and evening, I give thanks. If the transplant doesn't work, I will give thanks for this summer, for these last few months. If I look at it this way, how can I lose? No, the only question is how much more life, abundant and heaped and undeserved, I may be given.

When you dance out to meet your fate, you do not know whether it will swallow you whole or smile and send you on your way. Still you dance, you stomp, you twirl, you say, "Eat me if you dare, but I am going to keep on dancing!" Why not meet my fate with gusto and flair, eyes flashing, singing at the top of my lungs?

I watched a little girl, about five, pick up a large quahog shell with a hole in it and run back to show the two mothers walking behind her and the other children. "Look at this!"

The mothers nodded, admiring the shell. Satisfied, the little girl dropped it in the sand. "Jessie," called one of the women, "Take it with you. Take it home." Obediently the child ran back and put it in her pail. I felt I was witnessing some sort of morality play about possessions. The little girl had enjoyed the shell and was happy to let it go. Yet she was taught, "If you find something pretty it is not only your right but your obligation to possess it." What will the child do, the next time she finds a pretty thing?

I pause, in mid July, to wonder how I have changed since the early days of my diagnosis. I am more humble now than in December, more aware that I could tumble from life on short notice. I am less cocksure. But less full of faith? I don't think so. Faith is being tested and challenged—but I think it is no weaker. It is, if anything, becoming solid and strong. I am a little embarrassed about my former overconfidence. Yet I still call on my belief in abundance now that my life is twice as threatened. This is a good sign. I am still giving thanks for everything I have received when the situation is much, much worse. If I can keep this up, then there is no way to lose. The process itself is the outcome.

July 12

Randomness is the kick and the surprise of the universe, the clown, the unpredictable twist. Without it there would be far too many conscious decisions to make, and life would be a good deal less fun. To have play and unpredictability, we must also endure the tragic surprise, the cosmic practical joke, even the body's cells that flip the wrong switch and go haywire. But how else could one design a universe worth living in? Chaos is not an enemy; it can be a creative partner, if we discover that this demon is also a clown, and we dance with it. The task of cocreating the evolving world has to do not with eliminating chaos but with learning to dance with it more gracefully.

The random clown. It suddenly hit me—I know who this is! *Coyote, the Trickster.* Native Americans made him a character in their myths. They knew what mischief, even tragedy, he could cause, and told stories about him that made them laugh. The playful, unpredictable clownishness of the universe. For all the grief he brings, the universe would have no spunk without him.

What genius those myths contain. They tell that Coyote, the Holy Trickster, is also the creator of the world. Indeed, it is random genetic mutation—Coyote's tinkering—that allows for the evolution of life. It's also Coyote's random playfulness behind the "uncertainty principle," the outrageous law of physics that allows the possibility of an electron randomly jumping to the moon, against which Einstein protested, "God does not play dice with the universe." Apparently he does, and it keeps us on our toes.

It is disrespectful to Coyote to build a nuclear power plant on an earthquake fault, or place 50,000 nuclear weapons on a computer launch protocol. It is disrespectful to throw poisons into the sea, to smoke cigarettes, or shun seatbelts. To "tempt fate" is to taunt the random prankster and give him more power to do mischief.

July 16

A three-day break, and a blessed one. We drove straight from a radiation treatment to the Maine wilderness, spent two days close to the river, and then came straight back for the next treatment, without even going home. As we rode the rapids or slept in our familiar tent, I completely forgot I was sick. Going forward with life 100 percent feels so healthy and right. When I am going to the hospital every day and have the sore throat from the radiation, it is difficult to "forget" what is happening. But when I am with the river, and the fragrant cedar trees, and the sweet wild red raspberries along the banks, it comes easy.

I read aloud a chapter from *Little Tree* as we huddled in the tent with Rick and Amy and their nephew, and split four pieces of torte among five people in a way that could have served as a conflict resolution parable. David and I also had three hours alone on the lower Kennebec River with our inflatable canoe. We hit one large rapid at the beginning, and I was knocked so far backward that we almost capsized. Our wet suits made the ride comfortable and we enjoyed ourselves despite cool, cloudy weather. We're thinking of going north next weekend, too, and we're planning to spend as much time outdoors as possible in August and September.

July 17

Despite the grim face of my radiation doc, my tumor looks smaller on the films. "So far so good," he said. I told him I could run and hike again, then looked him right in the eyes and said, "Thank you for helping me." He grinned like an eight-year-old boy who'd just been given a lollipop.

Ten treatments down, and nearly a month before we'll hear any more news about how we are doing. Now that my symptoms have cleared, there's no way to gauge our progress. As Tak put it, we're looking at stars without a telescope. When the tumor was eleven centimeters it was made up of about a trillion cells. CAT scans and chest X rays allow one to see a tumor as small as a billion cells. Gallium scans or slides from a biopsy can identify a tumor of a hundred million cells. Some very fancy new antibody marker test is supposed to find a clump of one million cells. After that, it's pure guesswork—stars without a telescope. When I was clean on the gallium scan last spring, I could have had as many as a hundred million cancer cells, or only ten.

Before a transplant, I have to get back to a gallium clean state, and *then* take a knockout dose of chemo and radiation to bring me down to about ten thousand cells, a number my body has a good chance of handling on its own. Everyone may have a hundred, a thousand, ten thousand lymphoma cells in their bodies—there's no way to be sure.

The transplant should kill the marrow and therefore all my white blood cells, but it apparently doesn't kill them all, because somehow I will keep a "memory" of my old immunities to diphtheria, polio, and so on. Fascinating! After the transplant Tak will piggyback cytotoxic agents on hound dog antibodies that will sniff out my remaining tumor cells. He has other tricks up his sleeve, too. But the biggest, scariest hurdle is *qualifying* for my transplant—getting this tumor down to invisible in the next three weeks and keeping it that way.

Tak put me on the waiting list early because my situation is "urgent." The bone marrow "harvesting" operation is now scheduled for mid-to-late September. The autumn equinox, during the harvest festival—what could be a more auspicious time?

The voice of death has started speaking once again.

"And in my realms," she said, "you will feel a joy and gladness, deep change, immense relief. You will explore and delight in bodilessness, with the same courage and energy you had in your incarnate life. You will take on the challenge of being a helper from the other side; your presence will be felt by others. Then like one who has spent many happy hours in the desert, yet begins dreaming of mountains, you will begin to dream of being reborn. That will mean forgetting, humbling, suffering, repeating the lessons. Yet the longing will build and the time will come when you will ask to reenter life, to once again know the simple pleasures of sun on skin, to feel the river currents, to watch the sunset, to make love on the damp ground, and listen to the mockingbird."

Eleven treatments now. I have a delicate tan on my chest from the radiation, and the thinner skin lets the blue veins show through. Tomorrow I will pass the halfway mark.

July 18

Midmorning on the beach, after a successful downing of Muesli and pills. I woke stiff from many dreams, including a brief nightmare where I heard the wheeze. I took many long, clear breaths in the morning to assure myself it was only a dream.

I am tired from all these trips to the city, the weight of so many calls not made and letters not written. Who could imagine this would be such a busy time? I must allow two to three times more time as usual just to eat my meals because of my sore throat. And the chronic pain is a tiring presence. Yet this is a day for wonder, not complaint.

Here is my affirmation, my statement of hope:

"The radiation is working. The gamma rays are immensely powerful. The tumor is shrinking away. My body is strong and is recovering. I am healing. I am getting well."

I don't quite wholly believe this, but I almost do.

There is a "cancer shelf" in one of the Cambridge bookstores, and a quick look at it made me mad. I read a line at random in one volume. It said: "People who develop fast-growing, aggressive tumors have not learned how to find gratification within themselves, and still primarily seek the approval of others." I was immediately furious. What a crock! What a perversion of the wisdom that "choice matters" into "all that matters is our choice"!

On the shelf there were a few conspiracy books claiming that "doctors and bureaucrats have suppressed a known cure"; a number of books on cancer prevention that clearly play on people's fears; Bernie Siegel's helpful writings; and a technical guide or two. The prevention books droned on about "cancer-prone" personalities and "type C" people. Okay—tell people they can reduce their chances of getting cancer if they quit smoking, lose weight, eat healthy food, exercise, and live loving and fulfilling lives. But to talk of a "type C" personality implies "you brought this on yourself." The message is "you're guilty. You must change, repent." The fact is, there are millions of stressed, obese, smoking people who don't get cancer. These pop psychologists with their sloppy reasoning are scooped up by people desperate to make some sense of the question, "Why me?" People are attracted by the illusion of control: "You brought this on, so you can send it away." But this sets you up for guilt in a big way. And it's needless. I can't *control* whether or not I'll get well. But I can *choose* to line up all available healing forces on my side.

Then there's the other extreme. In a book of collected cancer stories, a doctor wrote: "I don't think attitude has anything to do with whether patients live or die. I've seen misanthropes do well. I've seen people surrounded by love and support go down the tubes." I'm sure he has, yet we can't conclude that attitude means nothing. Of course it doesn't work every time, but it does work sometimes. We will naturally notice when a curmudgeon lives and a loving person dies, because it strikes us as odd, as unexpected. But that's no reason to discount the power of prayer and will.

The beach was hot and glorious today, the shallow water warm enough to soak in. Despite my previous tiredness, I ran down the beach splashing at the water's edge. I pushed myself to go to the far rocks, where I swam in the cool deep water. It was a long run, the longest for me in months, perhaps even since I got sick—about two and a half miles in all. At the end, I sprinted.

July 19

In the radiation therapy waiting room today, two women with breast cancer were swapping stories. "God decides everything when we're born," the first one concluded. "Our fate is set, and we can't do anything about it." The other agreed.

That got me thinking. First of all, I don't believe fate and God are synonymous. There is more than one thing going on in this universe of ours! Second, it can be comforting to believe in predestination, but with that comes no responsibility and no triumph. It's all luck and fate. As Kushner points out, who would want a God like that? Who wants a world of zero uncertainty, where we act out the predetermined moves of someone else's game?

July 20

During a massage, I spoke lovingly to my body, telling it I was proud of its growing muscles, its healthy-looking tan, its returning strength. My body is bewildered by this tumor, and it has gotten the message something very drastic is about to happen—the marrow of the bones will be killed. It wants to know, is this a punishment? I spoke to my muscles, my blood, my bones, and reassured them they had done nothing wrong. I promised my body that it would recover quickly and be strong again. Even now, to the casual observer, my body radiates health. "I admire your endurance!" said a woman two days ago on the beach, when she saw me run.

When we think of bone, we tend to think of hard, dry, empty bone, of the protective shell, not the live pink elastic core, surrounded by material that is light and flexible, yet immensely strong and tough.

The marrow. The core. The hidden depths. Soft and rose-pink, like crushed flower petals, tender and fragile, protected by the shell of bone. The inner recesses. The most vulnerable and shielded organ of the body is also the most capable of regeneration, of simply growing back like a salamander's tail. This embedded essence can be taken out, then returned to the waiting cavities that have been scoured clean by fire. After it is removed and washed, this pink spongy substance will be compressed into a fifty-milliliter tube and then sent back through one of my biggest veins. It will travel back to the crevices and take up residence once more. How will it find its way? How will it know where to go and what to do? Who, in God's name, thought this procedure up? What chutzpah! What reverence! The transplant is a healing tool. I speak to my marrow and tell it that this temporary separation and pruning is necessary for new life. The essence will be preserved, the pattern will be maintained. The river may run dry for awhile, but it will flow into beautiful pools and rapids once again.

Bones. Crossed bones represent death and evil—we are afraid of bones. They are the last to decompose, the parts of us most likely to stick around and rattle in the closet or turn over in the grave. Yet our bones are our essence, the makers of blood, the givers of form. Bone dance, bone power. Bones: the closest things we have to roots.

July 22

New Hampshire. Hiking uphill and down through the greenleaf forests, swimming in mountain ponds. All is well except for the sore throat, which is so painful that I gave up on a banana and had to cut a scallop into twenty-four pieces just to get it down. It is a paradoxical time. On the one hand I am radiantly healthy and happy, tan and energetic. On the other I still have pain in my back, and more cough than I'd like. My radiation docs tell me, with reserve, that my tumor is "a little smaller." What a difference it would make if one of them bounced into my room and said cheerfully, "Everything is going very well!" Instead, they behave as if they are trying to conceal bad news from me. And the nurse, with her expressions of disbelief about my "sturdiness," makes me feel like some odd bug she's caught in her net.

July 24

Lying on the beach, a jar of applesauce in hand. Will baby food be next? It is a lovely, clear dry day as I look across the water to the Maine coast. David and I are so much in love, at times we are like teenagers. At others we feel so much older than before, with deeper roots and more heartwood. David understands these next three weeks are the most severe test of faith. I will have a CAT scan, X ray, and injection on August 12, and a gallium reading on August 15.

Tak will be on vacation so Dr. Caplan will give me the news. There are possible scenarios, ranging from the worst ("The chest tumor is still hot," "A few other spots are showing up," or "It's in your bones now") to the best ("No hot spots—it's as clean and cold as ice!").

I have eight more sessions with Zack the Zapper, my cyclotron (David suggested we name it Frank Zappa). Yesterday in the waiting room I talked with a woman with lymphoma. Dorothy is fifty-nine and had a bone marrow transplant two years ago. She sailed through fine, had two healthy years, but now the lymphoma is back in her lung and in her marrow. She kept saying to me, "Oh, you're going to be fine. You're going to be one of the cures, we can tell." My hair has thickened and filled in since I began radiation. It's schnauzer material once more, so furry my nurse couldn't resist petting it.

The doubt gremlin, as part of his nasty little game, dresses up in costume and tries to pretend he is my intuition. The little charlatan! If I allow him to stay in the dark he can muffle his voice and fool me for awhile. But then I shine the spotlight of my attention on him and poof! It's only the clumsy little doubt gremlin, trying to be mistaken for the queen.

The doubt gremlin whispers, "I have a bad feeling about this, and you should, too!" Even if his dire prediction proves true, it does not mean he had foreknowledge. The person who wakes up every morning and says, "It will rain today" is sometimes right, but not because he knows anything about the weather. It is the same with doubt gremlins, who say the same pessimistic things on all occasions.

July 25

The beach is wonderful, with its clean cool sand, the big sky, the cormorants and sandpipers. Yet how I long for something wilder. I feel pulled away from these rows of cottages, away from the motorboats and jet skis. I long for the crisp clean desert, for the exuberant silence and cold streams of the mountains. I would be happy never again to hear a car engine, see a swatch of asphalt, or smell gasoline. I feel crowded here and I know I will not be able to tolerate this much longer. Oh, I do listen to the cardinals and the mourning doves and the mockingbirds. I was amazed yesterday by the virtuosity of a catbird. I love each wildflower and my spirit stretches to the high arching branches of the bigger trees. It is not that this place has no beauty. But to think how beautiful and bountiful it must have been a hundred years ago! I feel too much sadness in this land to ever feel at home here. Henry David Thoreau would shudder and say this land is dead, or nearly so, and he would be right. The seed of life remains here and there is much that could be done to foster it. Yet so gratefully would I fling myself to the ground of the still healthy earth and take in the primeval silence.

Some of the "cancer prevention" books tell us we should be slowing down, living with less stress, and taking better care of our bodies in order to prevent cancer. But we should be doing this because it is how to live to our full potential, not because we want to avoid disease. Learning to love because we don't want to get sick is crazy. Learning to love in order to get results—because it will keep us healthy—is a trap. It is like trying to do good only because it is good for us. "Change, or you'll get sick!" the books say. It's exploitative to use fear of disease—the modern version of fire and brimstone—to get people to reform.

Ellen laughed yesterday when I described my two inner voices, one shouting: "Let go, let go, you have to release your attachment to life!" and the other, "Hang on! You have to fight for your life!" How do you let go of the cliff and hang on at the same time? Where is the place we can fight and surrender at the same time? The Buddhists say, "Accept, surrender, release." Bernie Siegel says, "Choose life and fight for it." Both are right; they are two sides of a paradox.

I went to my deck of animal cards and pulled Ant. I had to laugh when I read, "Ant eats slowly and deliberately." My throat is catching the full brunt of the radiation and eating is terribly painful. I have not been able to take my vitamins because I can't swallow cold liquids. It takes perseverance to eat soft egg salads, chicken soups, creamed spinach, applesauce. There is something mythic about it: I am hungry and presented with platefuls of tasty food, but I cannot eat.

A bad coughing spell tonight, and I tell myself it is an inflammation caused by the radiation. Just five weeks ago, a similar cough meant the chemo wasn't working. But this time I feel it really is nothing. If it is—we'll know by Saturday. Oh, the strength that is required at these times!

I thought of Dorothy, who had a recurrence after her bone marrow transplant. She could accurately be described by the medical profession as "someone who is dying." Yet she dresses in bright-colored pants and tops, in oranges and pinks. She is alert and lively. Bernie Siegel says you can only be alive or dead, not "dying." Good point.

July 28

The "evidence" we have for believing these treatments are working is thin, yet I hold on to it for dear life. I think of John Muir swaying in the top of a tree during a mountain storm. I try to feel his surging exhilaration as I sway in my own strong winds. My symptoms were gone after five treatments, my blood counts and overall energy are high (much higher and better than in mid June or May, during tumor-growth times). There is no wheeze, no gurgling. So I cling to the treetop and try to sing hosannas above the roaring storm.

July 29

We lay down our gifts on the altar of the Goddess, and she gives them back to us, to use in the world.

The path to her temple is steep and windy, with rounded rocks, damp moss clinging to the sides. The mountain is cool, fragrant, green beneath the mist. You smell the potent wet lilac and juniper, the pennyroyal and mint underfoot. Though you have climbed here with faith and courage in your heart, a shiver passes through you when you see the dark temple set into the mountain like a cave.

You are wearing green, and stones of purple around your neck—your hair is long and loose, curling slightly in the dampness. You feel your amulet bag against your chest, your medicine pouch and your knife at your waist. You reach the door and open it. Inside, there are fires and incense. A soft flute is playing. A large crystal is in the center of the room, surrounded by a ring of candles. You approach the crystal, place your hand on its smooth round face, and hear words:

"Do you come of your own free will?"

"Yes," you say. Then, wanting to be fully honest, you add, "And because it is my fate."

"Do you give up all you own to the service of the Goddess—to bring love, beauty, wonder, and creativity into the world that you have chosen?"

"Yes."

"What do you have to give?"

"I give my empathy. I give my poet's voice. I give my tenacity and endurance. I give my gift of clear thinking. I give my gifts as priestess and shaper of energy. I give my knowledge of song, dance, ritual, prayer, and magic."

"These are easy. What do you have that is difficult to lay down on my altar?"

"I give away my need to be acknowledged and appreciated. I give away my wish for success, comfort, and approval. My need to be right, to be in control. I give away my complaints and my self-pity. My fixed ideas about myself and about my future."

"Good," the voice says softly. "Is there anything else?"

"I give away my achievements." The next thing is hard to do, yet you know you must. "I give my life itself."

"Do you give up your love for others?" The question comes sharp and sudden.

"I do not give up my love for David, and for my dear ones. I give up my attachment to the forms love takes. But not the love itself."

"Will you obey me at all times, even if you must give up your own feelings and opinions?"

"No," you say, "I will listen, but I will not obey you blindly, without consulting my own true inner voice."

"Will you bind your hands, blindfold your eyes, and follow me wherever I lead you?"

"I will follow you," you say, "but with my eyes open, and my hands free. How else can I do your work? I am an extension of your wisdom and creativity, and you need me not as a slave or servant, but as a free-thinking and intelligent being. Through us, you become still more beautiful. You need our dreams and our actions to embody love and beauty in the world."

"My daughter," says the voice. "You have answered well. But there is much you do not know. There are risks on this path and the risks are real. I cannot protect you from pain or disappointment. I cannot tell you what will happen next. Do you still choose to give yourself to me, knowing this? There are other chambers, other gods, who promise certainty."

"I know these gods, but I choose you. Your temple is on a steep path, but it is filled with beauty."

"Go, my daughter," the voice says lovingly. "I give you my blessing and my love. You will find me in the sound of the ocean, in the wink of a falling star, in the song of a mockingbird, in the smell of sage and juniper, in the feeling of earth beneath your feet and wind on your skin. I am the smile in the eyes of people, the touch of passion playing between bodies. I am always near you. Your path is risky but beautiful. Go in peace, with a light heart. Go with the spirit of abundance, freedom, and gratitude. And remember who you truly are."

Physically, nothing has changed. But I am making some kind of shift, from trying to avoid death to trying to embody as much life as I can. In the five treatments I have left, I will no longer imagine the tumor melting away. I will visualize an enormous amount of light filling my body, filling it with health and love.

Even my dreams have changed. For three or four nights now I have been dreaming of myself as whole and healthy. Last night I dreamt I was on a table about to have my bone marrow transplant, but the whole thing was a joke and Tak leaned over to give me a kiss!

There is one problem with the advice "Live every hour as if it might be your last." Some things worth doing take time. If everyone lived this way, for example, no one would have babies. Children make you think about the future; they give you a horizon of time, a sense of continuity. Do you go ahead and get pregnant even though the odds are you won't last long enough to give birth? It is very well to say, "You've always wanted to be a violinist and you've got six months left, so play the violin!" But what if it takes two years to learn? What then? Do you fill your months with screechy practicing?

Our heart's desire takes time, preparation, training. What if your desire is to write a novel? It's not easy to embark on such a project if this day may be your last. The mind says, "If that's really true, you'd be better off singing, dancing, making love, walking on the beach—fulfilling those desires that can be satisfied in an hour." I face a curious paradox. I am living fully and joyously, though one of my deepest desires is to write books. It doesn't feel right to begin them; they demand a sense of future time. Is this just an excuse?

July 30

My radiation docs have changed their minds about the dose and have decided to scrap the last two treatments. So I have only today and tomorrow left. The throat got its last dose yesterday—a good thing, given that even lentil soup and applesauce go down hard.

In anticipation of the bone marrow transplant, Roy gave us the consent form for total body irradiation and we talked it over. These forms seldom tell you what good the treatment will do, only the horrible things that might happen, such as the sterility, which I had assumed. I had even heard something about cataracts. The rest seems like the usual chemo stuff—nausea, mouth sores, hair loss, etc. Yet also included in the horror list is "brain dysfunction, liver, kidney, or bladder abnormalities."

In the bone marrow transplant, I'll be receiving the equivalent of about six of my regular radiation zaps over my entire body. As Tak put it, it's the rough equivalent of standing one mile from ground zero in Hiroshima. However, people in Hiroshima did not have healthy marrow stored in a freezer! I asked if I will be able to walk from my transplant room to the radiation department, and was told I will go by ambulance the fifty yards between Dana-Farber and the Brigham Hospital. What comedy!

Somehow I can't take all of this very seriously. I am healthy as a horse, with fabulous blood counts and dreams of wholeness. Even David has started feeling more optimistic.

The marquee in front of the North Shore Assembly of God always gives me a lift when we pass it on the drive to the hospital. Some of the sermon titles are straightforward, like last week's "Regeneration" and this week's "Action of the Holy Spirit." Some are intriguingly mysterious, even a bit gothic: "Son of Perdition" and "The Rent Veil." My all-time favorite, so far, is this: "10:30 A.M.: Access to God." Access—the key word of the nineties!

July 31

Today is the last day of treatment.

Am I really so alone, without help, when the treatments are over? I have so many people praying, the medicine has blasted the heck out of the tumor for nearly five weeks—3,800 rads is no skimpy dose! I have the additional support of vitamins, good food, the fresh air. If only the docs would say something genuinely reassuring, if only I didn't know how quickly this thing can "roar back." In order not to let these terrors pester me to distraction, I need to believe—whether it is "true" or not—that the tumor is gone.

EVENING

Radiation is over! (No more until the transplant!)

I didn't flinch when Peter Mauch came back into the room after examining my films and asked curtly, "What are you doing next week?" "Going on vacation," I said. He pondered this for some time, frowning. Why would he want me back if the news were good? He said it was a tough call whether to give me two more treatments. Then he said, "Let's finish today."

"Well," I said, "I feel good, and my counts are great, so I think it's going well!"

"Oh yes," Peter said, "you've responded nicely."

David and I looked at each other.

"It's nice to hear you say it." I felt tears in my eyes.

In retrospect, I had so many defenses up that I could hardly absorb the good news. These smart technicians didn't have to wait five weeks to give us some encouragement, dammit!

Recently the doubt gremlins have been saying, "The tumor might have spread to sites not treated by radiation!" But yesterday's good news quiets them some. I feel an urge to celebrate, but to do so quietly and privately: This turning of the tide is too precious and vulnerable to tell others yet.

I am only just beginning to realize the great strain of the last two months. For just a moment the powerful winds in which I have become accustomed to living—winds that seem capable of flinging me off the earth—have died down a bit. I feel more anchored here. I look at the world with more belief that I will stick around for a while. But it is, as yet, only a very slight lull. Enough to make me realize how tugged and pulled I've been. Toes and fingers wedged into the rock, the rest of me dangling in the hurricane.

August 1

Today is the old Celtic holiday of Lammas, the midpoint between summer solstice and fall equinox, a pregnant time of year.

> *We stand now between hope and fear, in the time of waiting. In the fields, the grain is ripe but not yet harvested. We have worked hard to bring many things to fruition, but the rewards are not yet certain . . .*
>
> —Starhawk, *The Spiral Dance*

> *A lot can happen between now and gathering, and the crops are promising but not yet secure . . . What [we] asked for at the Summer Solstice spiral dance is ready to happen.*
>
> —Diane Stein, *Casting the Circle*

Lammas is the festival of first harvest, of first fruits, and here we are, celebrating the first small taste of good news. There are still weeks before the final harvest and many things could happen, but we are grateful for having made it this far.

It has been hard work, and David and I are ready for a vacation. A solid eleven days "off," a respite from the hospital. But not a "break" for any cancer cells that might still be alive within me, of course. Only a switch in therapy, from allopathic sabers of gamma rays to conscientious diet, laughter, fresh air, silence, trees, wild creatures on their nests. Vacation therapy!

Before I plunge into the water, I call not just to the ocean but to something that is immanent and embodied in the ocean. What is this presence I invoke? It is also in the fire, the winds, the soils and rocks, in the call of owl and the song of the dove, in the saxifrage and the rose, the gaze of the wolf, the grace of deer, the gesture of kindness between people. It is an enduring consistency that I feel compelled to call by a name. I recognize it as the Goddess, knowing all the while that this sameness of pattern cannot be taken away from context, from form, from the immanent reality.

August 4

I am writing by flashlight in the dome tent, on the edge of the forest in a far corner of Maine, camping with Mom. We have seen carnivorous pitcher plants and sundew, wet furry beds of moss, spectacular cliffs and coves. Five miles of walking helped calm a vague anxiety that has been with me since I left. Perhaps it's the sudden separation from David, or Mom's talking so much about other places and other times that it underscores how much I've been living in the here and now. I have wanted, often, just to be silent, to be with what beauty and stillness we can find, and I realize how expert David is at leaving me alone and giving me this kind of solitude.

A single loon calls from across the water—loon lullabies. This wet, half-dripping silence of soaked lichens and spongy trees is ideal for deep sleeping.

I do miss David. We have not been apart since February, so it is something of a jolt. Still, there is one thing I am constantly grateful for: My breaths are deep and silent.

August 5

A day that began discouragingly, with a twenty-five-knot east-nor'easter, no hope for puffins, soaked tent and leaky raincoat. But once we found a haven at the Home Port Inn, the day improved. We managed an afternoon excursion across the border to Canada for a spectacular, soggy, four-mile walk. The quiet, stark, rain-soaked ocean cliffs are reminiscent of Oregon or Northern California. Would our own Massachusetts coast look like this if it were not suffocated by houses and asphalt?

Having hung clothes to dry, I'm catching up here in my journal. One small thing I have learned: People who have not faced the imminent possibility of death are like diners trying to describe the taste of lobster based on what lobster looks like. Last week at my dance group I heard some old clichés which were said rather lightly: "Death is just a transformation," and "We're all stardust, after all." I felt a voice within me protest: "That's easy for you to say when you're not facing the prospect of becoming stardust rather soon!" It was not the content of the remarks but their casualness. These things are true but they are hard truths, glinting and sharp like chipped obsidian.

Slugs! Wet yellow slugs, two inches stretched out, along the trail. The creative source did not stop with the big obvious beauties like whales but went on to produce slugs, slime molds, shelf fungi, huge curved-tailed mayflies, cavernous maws of hungry pitcher plants.

The rafts of molting eider ducks waft into the sea when they sense our approach on the high cliff.

August 6

MACHIAS SEAL ISLAND, MAINE

It is healing to see the earth so shimmeringly full of life on this island. The thousands of birds, the rise and fall of tern-song, the abundance strikes us as uncommon only because we have grown so accustomed to living in a biologically impoverished place. This was the norm for almost all of time, this teeming abundance, these swells of disparate songs, these intricate colonies of tribes peaceably intermixed. Here, the pallor of our world is obvious. Twenty years ago, our Gloucester beach was covered with horseshoe crabs; we are lucky to find one or two today. The bobwhite and bobolinks have disappeared from the Ohio farm where I was raised. And this was only the tail end of the great silencings of this century. Can I imagine our marsh in Gloucester filled with geese and other birds, live and cackling, like this lonely island nine miles offshore?

The terns are embodiments of the warrior spirit—loud, aggressive, insistent, all slender points and sharp edges, with blood-red bills and feet. They defend the island, keeping the black-backed gulls at bay so that puffins and auks may nest. The auks (razorbills) are elegant, dignified, coordinated, and social. The puffins all seem very, very old, preoccupied with deep questions. Their clown faces have a kind of solemn hilarity achieved only by the wise. They fly like parrots, feet splayed and flattened, stubby wings whirring, as if it took them a good deal of effort. The terns adroitly carry silver herring balanced tightly in their beaks, yet the puffin's ready-made slots hold up to four fish at once. At times the terns shove their wing shoulders forward, arch their backs, and point thin tails to the sky.

The rocks smell richly of guano. The tall lush grasses are filled with aster, yarrow, wild carrot, buttercup, and are humming with bees, flies, admirals, and monarchs. Butterflies, my symbol of transformation! A monarch caught the boat draft and followed for a while. Bobolinks, yellow warblers, cowbirds, cliff swallows, savannah sparrows, dowitchers, turnstones, spotties, gannets, blue heron. A minke whale turns to the west, and fifty yellow-silver harbor seals watch us from the cool safety of the water. It is alive, I tell you—an orchestrated song, alive as the planet is meant to be alive, healthy and bellowing hosannas to the morning.

What joy it will be, to those who come after us, to listen to the songs return more loudly to the wounded places of the Earth, to see the stillness begin to move and dance once again. There are so many opportunities for heroism today. One hero is the man who patiently re-established a puffin nesting colony on a Maine island. The heroism needed to restore, to nurture, to undo the damages and let the wounds heal is so enormous and so appealing.

Last night, I suddenly awoke with a startling thought: If I don't live through the transplant, this is my last time to be with the healthy, living Earth. I felt fear enter my bed and creep under the covers. I have not learned any surefire panaceas for eliminating this kind of sadness. I suspect there are none.

For a few days I have been wondering whether my medicine name could be Dancing Eagle. How does one get confirmation on these things these days? Where are the medicine women who would know? We have to become them, ourselves.

August 7

Another blessed day spent in healthy land—or healthy, anyway, in this narrow corridor of the river, snaking between clear-cuts. The river itself is wild and genuine. River days always leave me relaxed, sun-soaked, loosened. The moment of hanging just before a big drop, the sucking boom of crashing into a wave, the toss up over a standing haystack, the meeting of muscle, paddle, and water. I could do it all day, every day. At the end of the day I always mourn the last rapid, but I leave content.

A spotted sandpiper bobs on a midriver rock. Our guide gave me one precious piece of data today: mergansers run rapids for the fun of it, just like the rafters do, careful to hold their course, grinning as they go down into frothing holes. He has seen them, however, apparently change their minds at the last moment and hop into the air just before a particularly big wave.

After swimming in the river, I had trouble getting back to the boat and heard, in my rapid deep breaths, sounds I did not like. I heard them again after a long stretch of paddling, a few minutes later.

I've got to play a hard defensive game a little longer. I concentrate and fill my lungs, silently now, with the clean river air.

August 8

A song I learned at the sacred circle dance:

> The river, she is flowing—
> Flowing and growing.
> The river, she is flowing
> Down to the sea.
>
> Mother, carry me—
> a child I will always be.
> Mother, carry me
> Down to the sea.

The river is both changeless and changing. Here in the wilderness, experiences, feelings, thoughts flow through me. My life is like the river: It adds to itself, grows, becomes stronger and more lovely. I am also like a stationary wave in the river; water flows through me, but I remain. I am an enduring pattern, one among trillions in a vast interlocking pattern of waterways.

Tonight, speaking on the phone to David, I was overcome by the strength of our love. I need to be held by him, for a long time, and I need to cry. I must feel my intense anguish in order to be renewed and calm again. The shadows flicker on the wall, the doubt-gremlins keep whispering "Do you hear something in those fast deep breaths? Do you? Do you . . . ?" How much I want to live, how much I want to stay here with David. I don't want to die! So simple, this phrase which I have never before uttered. This is the shadow side, inevitable and natural, of the powerful affirmation, "I choose to live."

The flowers have already bloomed. The end of summer approaches. A time of pods and burrs and swellings. Dark, leathery leaves, growth nearly stopped. A waiting time, before the harvest.

August 14

Six days is an eon of experience. Family have come and gone. Yuri, Lena, and Anya, visiting from Moscow, are sleeping on the futon. Yesterday was a wild morning full of family and kids, cello and flute duets, a circle dance. We awoke in astonishment to find Frank and his German friends had pitched their tent in the front yard. High waves had forced their kayaks off the sea. Windblown but happy, they ate doughnuts and applauded our dance performance.

My parents, too, were visiting. I had a long, pleasant walk with them to the rocks at the end of the beach. As we said good-bye, David took Dad aside, and said, "We aim to win."

On Monday, the CAT scanner broke and my CAT was postponed; then we learned that Tak broke his neck while bodysurfing. Thank God, he doesn't seem to have any neurological damage, but he is in a halo for twelve weeks with several broken cervical vertebrae—nasty stuff! He will probably be fine, but he came nearer to death than I have been. Poor Tak. His last comment to *me* was not to fall out of the boat in Maine and hit my head on a rock.

While I worried about Tak, David worried about me and possible delays in my treatment. We arranged to meet Debbie Toppmeyer, who is covering for Tak. She was reassuring, had my history down cold, and convinced us that I would not fall through any cracks. "None of us can pretend to fill Tak's shoes," she said, "but this is a small, tight-knit place and we believe in continuity of care." She seemed to know everything about me, and left us with the impression that Arnie Freedman—the transplant doctor—did as well. They'd already put their heads together and cooked up a new chemo recipe for me.

August 16

Last night, a voice came to me saying one word: *Trust.* I listened to this voice as I numbly set the table, and something tight in me—something I had imagined would only be loosened when I lay in David's arms and cried—began to come apart. It is time to let go, to trust I am being taken care of in ways I know nothing about, and cannot even imagine. Trust that I am loved and cherished. Trust that no matter what, things will be all right.

There are terrifying hints of new tumors and we don't know if they are real. But when I ask, "Will I be okay, no matter what?" the voice answers, "Yes," loosening the fear that was bound so tightly around my spirit that I could hardly breathe. This gentle, commanding voice had said to the fear-gremlins, "Let her go. Leave her alone." And they did. I began to feel better. I no longer even wanted to cry.

Just before the scan yesterday, I looked in the mirror and thought: I am nervous, but not really afraid. I wanted so badly to be told, "You're clean!" Oh, the party that should have been! My awesomely clean and ice-cold chest was ruined by some dark spots in my belly. Shadows on the wall? An illusion cast by technology and all that remains mysterious in the body? One spot, at least, might be explained as normal elimination of the gallium. But the other is rather high, near the gall bladder and ribs. "They may disappear on the followup scan, and be nothing," said Caplan. "Worst case, you have two little ditsals of disease." Would I still qualify for a transplant?

I wanted reassurance from my doctors. They said, "We don't know yet if these spots are *real*, so don't worry about it." What I wanted to hear was, "Even if they are real, we still believe you can get well." Arnie Freedman said, "This sounds like a red herring." But when we pressed him with questions, he said that if the spots are real, I'd have to shrink them down before they'd give me a transplant, otherwise "the transplant would be pointless." In other words, if things went badly from now on, he'd give up on me.

Now I am coming to a new place, where I must consciously choose to believe something different than my doctors. I read in Arnie's eyes, "If this lady has gone Stage III, she's not going to make it." When I am less off-balance I will be able to say, "Arnie, I expect to get well, and I need you to believe this, too."

Later, Debbie examined me. My breathing was a little constrained, and my heart rate unusually fast. I told her I was scared. She took my hand and encouraged me to think positive and not dwell on the worst. I thanked her, tears swelling in my eyes. I was glad I had been so honest and so vulnerable. It was the first time I'd told any of my doctors I was frightened.

This morning I lie in the dawn light and feel calm and peaceful. If I can just keep that feeling, all will be well. The idea of tumors in my belly seems outlandish. I put my hands there and get no inkling of disease. Even if there is cancer there now, it's not a real problem. It won't slow us down in the long run. This is my gut instinct. I place my hands on my belly and trust. I trust that I can get well.

August 17

MORNING, THE WHITE MOUNTAINS, NEW HAMPSHIRE

It is curious that when the doctors start feeling beleaguered, I would begin to feel such calm. I am going to survive, I am going to get well! I have enormous faith in my next chemo round. I am so receptive and eager for this help, so willing to work in partnership with these drugs.

For two and a half months I have been holding a demanding yoga posture, enjoying the long stretch, breathing through the pain. It takes a great deal of effort, and at the same time releases such intense joy. I thought that on Thursday I would be able to relax and release, to move into a restful counterpose. But this was not to be.

Instead I am being asked to reach even further, to stay with the stretch and find a new level of peace. More effort and more joy: a deepening.

Meanwhile people all over the world, many of whom I do not even know, are holding healing circles and saying prayers for me. As far away as Holland, Sweden, and Czechoslovakia. Each prayer matters, each one is a loop of thread tying me a little more securely to the tree, to the wet firm bark. Each one holds me here a little longer, as the winds pick up, the rain soaks my hair, runs into my eyes, and washes my body clean.

August 18

Yesterday we climbed up 2,000 feet to the breathtaking summit of Mount Osceola. We lay together in a secluded glade on soft green moss, and breathed in the essence of trees, rocks, lichen, waxwings. We climbed down and with every step I felt more assured. It is a time to hook in as many belay lines as possible, tethers to the cliff. Our doctor friend Gerry threw a line tonight when he told me, in his medical experience, each case is so unique that "bad signs" mean nothing.

PART THREE

purifications
with
water and fire

August 19

This is a big day in the world and my own history—a hurricane, a coup in Moscow, and the return of the cancer—and I feel I must mark it with at least a few words, a genuflection of some kind, an "Oh, wow!"

The hurricane turned out to be nothing and our tomatoes lived. At present I believe I also will live, and people in the Soviet Union will pull through as well. Perhaps this is all stubborn, wild-eyed, Ohio farm girl optimism, but it's what I feel just now. There's a media blackout in Moscow. People are in the streets facing down tanks with an impossibly strong desire to not yet give up hope. We sent an electronic message to our partners there, and our phone is ringing off the hook at home.

We also discovered a hot peanut in my liver and four other ditsals (the official word) scattered through my lung, spleen, ribs, and liver backside. I'm at Dana-Farber, and the chemo is going into me just now, while in Moscow people are singing at the barricades and lighting bonfires in the night. A helluva day.

Tak is sedated but still consulting in my care. We are pinning our trust on VP-16, isophosfamide, carboplatinum—go to it, guys! Put out those fires and let us get on with things! I'm now Stage IV, multiorgan involvement. But all these dots are considered "minimal disease," with no systemic symptoms. Still, everything must now be mobilized. Everything. If we hold steady, at least, I can be transplanted, and the statistics say extranodal and minimal disease status does not affect the long-term outcome.

In the midst of my crisis I keep wondering what is Gennadi doing? Volodya? Slava? Zhenya and the girls? What about Irina, and Lyuba, and Nadia, and Galina? Don't lose heart, don't lose courage, dear ones, don't believe you have already lost. You are your own people, you don't have to accept a hopeless destiny. Feel the warrior spirit rising within you! On the one hand, I am very healthy; on the other I am very, very sick. The same is true for you. The first chemo is in, and your first night at the barricades has begun.

August 20

Igor has sent us three courageous e-mail messages, one just before leaving for the rally at the Russian Parliament building. Rumors that troops were closing in have so far amounted to nothing. Our friends in Moscow spent all night running off pamphlets on methods of nonviolent protest. Thousands are mobilized, with courage coming not only from fear but also from love.

On this side, the first batch of chemo went in safely. No big problems, only the nuisances of hospital noise, fluorescent lights, constant interruptions, and no privacy. It is so difficult to remain centered and calm. Yet I have stored up so much in preparation for this that I have plenty to carry me through.

My counts are somewhat low, my LDH level high . . . there is lymphoma unquestionably simmering throughout my body, yet somehow, with love and serenity, I am not sick. I believe these new sites began growing around solstice, and that all the prayers, all the river trips, all the hikes, all the dancing, all the healing circles, all the writing since kept them tiny and in check. My beloved body, how I wish I could put you in a quiet, restful sanctuary, play you beautiful music, and turn all my concentration toward amplifying the flow of blood and helping drugs get to these tiny tumors and wash them away.

EVENING

Oh, how fragile life seems, at times—these frail human bodies and buses propped against Soviet Army tanks. And little transparent bags of chemicals flowing into my body, stubborn little forces powered almost wholly by belief. All are battling such huge unconscious things. It will be a long night.

Lying in the park today, on a two-hour pass, I suddenly realized that the body is not a sausage packed densely with discrete organs, but rather a continuous whole, an intricate sack of interweaving fluids, of pulses and ebbs and flows, a spiral dance, a swirling galaxy, everything absolutely intimately awash in everything else. And into this swirl of current and dancing structures the healing drugs have come, gently soaking the whole light-filled, humming entity. I think of the Queen Anne's lace I used to pick and stick into jars of food coloring; the unnatural but lovely blues, greens, and pinks would gently suffuse and transform the flowers into something very different.

August 21

What a beautiful day!

On television I watch the tanks leave Moscow. Tears come to my eyes, and I thank God I have lived to see this. All morning, as the celebration filled me, shivers passing through my core, I could not help but think: The attempted coup in my body is also being routed, the lymphoma tanks are retreating, the power of love and connection and will is winning.

I am so tired, and so TV-burned, that I must try to sleep. I have no poetry in me, only numb relief. I watch in wonder as the soldiers are gaily waving and calling out, "We are leaving, we are leaving, we are leaving forever."

August 25

What a week. The events of the world churned through me, steamed a passage, and my own thoughts fled for the banks. Now, at last, things are quieting. David and I were both pushed to emotional and physical limits. But finally I'm home, letting the warm sand soak up the stress. I've seen three men carrying babies today, up and down the beach, and this cheers me.

Shots of growth factor in the leg, each evening, are still a bit startling. Miracle-Gro for the bone marrow! A sumptuous turkey dinner and pumpkin pie for my tired and hungry marrow cells. My body, without question, is one baffled sack of liquid structures, as mellow as kelp in the current, tugging and shifting and accommodating every wave. Months of IVs should have disabused me of the classic snap-together plastic model of the body's innards from high school biology, where veins are solid and discrete. There's no getting around the permeability of every boundary and border. I take a tiny needle and stick it in a half inch—incredibly, and this is the point, almost anywhere—into the layer of flowing fat just under my skin. The soft wads obligingly move aside, so that only a small lump forms and that soon disappears. Within the hour, this small tumbler of goodies will be distributed in great osmotic egalitarianism throughout this delicate, pulsing sack I inhabit.

August 28

Next, a platelet count of 14 and a trip to the Farber for a transfusion, painful hemorrhoids, a slight fever, a sore throat. White count at rock bottom 0.3. Whoops! I lay on the futon and thought cooling, stilling thoughts. David came up with a theory for the throat—incipient thrush—and we began to treat it. I roused myself to drink and eat, and spent the evening with a good three-hour movie, *Sherman's March*. The fever stabilized, even dropped a bit, to 99.2. I slept with more confidence, and after the usual hospital trip (platelets hanging in there at 36) came here to the beach. It's rough sailing, as Tak had said on the phone. Going to Jeff and Barb's wedding in Seattle three days from now may be impossible. At the moment it is a triumph merely to be here and not in the hospital. Go, megakaryocytes—make those platelets! Poor dears, I have given them such a rough time. I'm scheduled for a transfusion of red blood cells tomorrow, and that should bring a burst of new energy. One day at a time? One hour at a time is more like it.

The possibility of yet another round of chemo raises questions in our minds. This would delay the transplant two to four weeks, at least. Should we really sit around waiting for trouble to brew? Is that a decision based on what's best for me, or on the flow of beds in the unit? Why all these extra tests to "prove myself"—when I qualify even now? It is a tricky situation, and we feel Tak's absence. Part of me just wants to trust the new doctors and let them decide. But my body will accept another round of chemo far more graciously if we fully understand all the reasoning behind it. If the idea is, "another round of chemo will put you farther ahead for the transplant," then okay. This is all assuming that the chemo in me now is working. I've lost three out of four of my pitons on this climb, but I've still got one solid one, and every reason to think it will hold. With one piton or four, you can still get to the top safely. You just can't lose that fourth piton, that's all. "Yours is made of kryptonite," Mark Dubois lovingly told me this morning. "Of course it will hold!" So we baby the blood and body along, with sunshine, seawater, and hope.

Today I began to imagine what the actual process of dying might be like. The letting go of everything and saying good-bye. I had just a few glimpses: flowers by the bedstand, packing for the hospital knowing it could be for the last time, the final phone calls. As much as I've thought about death, I had never had any images of the process. Today I even began to think about how I would arrange it to my liking. The music, the people around me, what I would say to them. Clearly I am going to deeper levels of acceptance of a possible premature departure. Yet with this is also coming a curious sort of optimism. More and more, I feel I am going to survive against the odds. I know I am doing my part to dance out to the edge of fate. I know I am doing everything possible, and I feel peaceful and clear about this. Leaving the rest up to God is starting to feel very, very good.

Tak and I spoke Wednesday, my third day in the hospital—the first of several nice things to happen that day. He called me, and he sounded quite cogent despite his pain pills, and touchingly open about how he felt. "I'm trying to figure out why I was spared," he said. "I should have been a quadriplegic—I came within one millimeter of that. And then I found out I had broken my odontoid, which means I should have been dead." His rational, medical mind can find no explanation for why he is alive and healthy—and so he is facing the most profound of mysteries. Why are there miracles sometimes, but not *all* the time? For some people but not everyone? Why was there a miracle for me? He told me, "I almost would rather have suffered the logical consequences, and *know* why it happened than have no explanation." I told him my assessment of my situation—how the new "ditsals" would not mean much in the long term. Unless the doctors here were hiding something from me, the general feeling seemed to be we'd weather this fine. "Of course, it would have been nice to celebrate clean scans now," I said.

"So you'll get to do that in a few weeks," he replied. "How you *feel* is very important. We have every reason to be confident this round will work." Then he tested me a bit for signs of discouragement: "I tried to warn you that this might happen." I reassured him that I felt very good about the choices we had made, and I told him that I missed him. His voice cracked. He said, "I feel like I've let you down." I reassured him gently, telling him I knew he was still there for me. He regained his composure and said that I was really not being taken care of by him but by the Farber—a collective organism of amazing intelligence.

"The most important thing you have done for me, Tak, is that you've always believed I can get well."

"Oh yeah," he replied, with such easy honesty in his voice that I could've kissed him. He really does believe that still. We patients, in some ways, ask for so little from our doctors—it is worth so much just to be told, "I believe you can make it. I believe you can do it." We don't need guarantees, just a willingness to hope at our sides.

I told him about David's dream in which he was healed and well, with a fully mobile neck. "It seems impossible to imagine now," he said. "Sometimes I have trouble believing this will be over, too," I said, "yet it will be, and *we'll both* be fine."

The days in the hospital passed. The routine always seems both so familiar and so odd, so unpleasant and so bearable . . . the little indignities of having to call for help to dress or undress, to pee in the little white hats, to untangle the lines from the wheels of the IV pole, to plug and unplug my IV pump, Fred-the-Imed, who had a stubborn tendency to spiral rather than roll in a straight line. I treasure the unhooked minutes of bathtime because I can close the door and achieve at least a small privacy from the constant flow of people. My roommate was absolutely glued to the television from 8:30 A.M. to 10:30 P.M. I was discomfited enough by her bowel leavings and vomit in the bathroom, but it was the TV that nearly killed me. If it hadn't been for the Soviet crisis, which kept me glued to the TV quite a bit, too, I would have insisted on a transfer.

On the twelfth floor of the hospital, David and I found refuge in a lovely meditation and prayer room with stained glass depicting trees, flowers, and butterflies. I felt as if I had stumbled into a chapel of the future where symbols of the divine reflect the beauty of the Earth. Later, I walked around the transplant unit and read the beautifully calligraphed instructions on the door telling visitors to wash, gown, and glove, and only bring in objects that have been sterilized. A nurse asked if she could help us, and we explained I would be coming here soon. The rooms are spacious—double rooms made into singles—and facing mostly west, a few to the south or north. In my mind I have already begun to fill mine with paintings, meditation bells, a tape deck and VCR, my most beloved clothes, computer and modem, Rolodex, and books.

I've been thinking about last week's hurricane. By satellite it was a gorgeous whirling spiral galaxy. When David drove home that night, he was struck by the way limbs and branches were strewn everywhere, "as if the earth and the sky had just had a wild passionate lovemaking session—the sheets strewn on the floor, books knocked over, clothes flung to the corner—and now in the air was a great calm freshness of total orgasmic release." I thought of Mon-o-lah in *Little Tree*, how the Cherokee believe she sends heavy storms in order to clean and prune the forests of all but the strongest limbs and trees, so that the whole will be healthier, and I knew I would never look at torn limbs with sadness again.

August 30

I'm at home now, but there have been many close calls and near trips to the hospital. Two nights ago was scariest of all. After a day on the beach, swimming, walking four miles, suddenly my temp started going up—100.5, 100.6. I tried to sleep but couldn't. It was up to 100.8—damn. I wanted to break the thermometer. I lay on the futon in the moonlight and went through the entire scenario in my mind: waking up David, driving to the hospital, the hour-long admission exam, the IV. I spoke to God: "Can't you just cool me off a couple tenths of a degree?" I visualized the moonlight entering my body, cooling and soothing, and in twenty minutes I took my temp again. It had dropped to 100.6. I waited a bit more: 100.5. Good heavens, I thought, it's working. I took a Halcion and finally slept at 3:00 A.M. I was playing with fire. The threshold for reporting to the hospital is 100.5.

Yesterday I was tanked up with blood and platelets, and hives swelled in great pink patches in my armpits, groin, and knees. A transfusion reaction. They rushed in fifty milligrams of Benadryl by IV and the hives died down, but it's not been my best week.

There have been times when I've felt tired of being sick. Humbling times. The body feels strangely hollow and fragile, even when I don't have a fever. Today the blood tests show my white count and platelets are slightly higher; maybe it means the marrow is starting to recover from the last round of chemo. If so, then there's still a remote chance we might be able to fly to Seattle tomorrow for Jeff and Barb's wedding. Our friend Brad has arranged for blood counts and a platelet transfusion in Seattle if necessary. What will make the difference is my white cell count. At any moment, my white cells could begin to soar upward, thanks to all the Miracle-Gro I've been injecting into myself. The idea of a trip to Seattle is pure play, a complete lark. Sometimes I think I must be crazy to even consider it. We've told Jeff and Barb we are definitely not able to come. But there is one more day for my marrow to shift into high gear. So go, marrow, go!

The day after I got out of the hospital last week, I managed to rouse myself and walk to the beach. This cheered me a great deal. I reached the beach just as the late sun hovered directly over the surf line, illuminating the foam with golden light, casting a path before me. As I walked toward this golden path it retreated before me, so that I never actually stepped on its radiance. When we die, I realized, the golden path no longer retreats: It waits for us, and we keep walking, firmly, closer to the source of light.

August 31

FLYING TO SEATTLE

Alternate futures—alternate realities. So swiftly we move forward with the current between the rocks of choice and chance, and find ourselves in a different place.

And here we are, incredibly, flying west over the Montana–Idaho border. A miracle that would not have happened had I strictly followed the rules. I would, instead, still be in Dana-Farber, hooked up to antibiotics, longing for the sea.

Lying on the airplane seats, I thought: Of course we'll be able to imagine our way to health. Just as we imagined our way out of the cold war, out of nuclear war before 1991 . . . sheer, gutsy, active imagination. The alternate futures were real, were so imaginable, too, and are still vividly imaginable as alternate pasts—but we did it, we hung in, we looked it square in the eye and chose otherwise.

Hope: taut with the awareness that no outcome is guaranteed—the awareness that the other, darker alternatives could still be entered, noiselessly, slippingly, if we let up on our love . . . yet always, even in the most improbable of times, believing yes.

September 2

When we arrived in Seattle we drove straight to the Cascade Mountains to the camp where the weekend-long wedding gathering had already begun. Margaret met us outside, then announced a "commercial break" in the skit that was in progress. We walked in. The looks of amazement on people's faces were so intense as to resemble horror—as if we had just appeared at our own funerals. After this moment of frozen astonishment, we dissolved into a sea of hugs and kisses, with squeals of delight and camera flashes.

At least ninety things could have prevented us from getting to the ceremony, including my platelet count, done at a lab down the road, that was barely high enough to keep me out of the hospital. But we were fully present. Barb's radiant face, Jeffrey's solemn intention.

That night: swing dancing, then the sweat lodge. "I love looking at all these naked bodies!" exclaimed Nina. We chanted and raised our arms to the sky and stars.

It was raining and cold, but in Margaret and Dan's spare sleeping bags we were safe and warm. We slept to the river hum and stooped to bathe at the water's edge in the morning.

As I sat cross-legged on the boughs in the sweat lodge, fragrant and close to sister and brother bodies, blood let loose from my womb, flowing onto the spruce and fern, running down to the damp earth. Only today the sad thought came to me—my last blood, I gave to the river.

The river water washed this warm sticky gift, mixed with spruce and fir needles, into the night current. The fire, the river, the damp cool soothing earth, and my body—the differences between them blurred. I was stunned with gratitude, and unafraid. My body opened in a movement born of its own wisdom, its own homage and worship. It was a spontaneous convulsion of joy, a hosanna it could not keep within.

Trust me, says the voice of the body. We revere the same things: the fire and the stones, the fir boughs and stars. There is harmony between us.

There are so many allies, dark, secret, and knowing, in the body. Never in all this have I been resentful of my body, never have I felt anything but tender compassion for its sufferings and partnership with its strengths.

September 3

We took a walk today in the Cascade Mountains. I was being told, "Remember the dry warm sunshine, cool wet feet on river-smooth stone, the dark walls of fragrant trees. Remember the snow-skinned face of the mountain."

We love mountains because they are the earth itself lifted grandly before our eyes. To love the flat prairie and forest takes more effort and imagination. But mountains make loving the earth, marveling at the bony beauty of our planet, easy.

Wilderness is where you can strip, swim, and sunbathe naked without fear. I immersed myself into the icy mountain stream, and lay on the stones, legs spread to the noon sun, bleeding onto the rocks, thighs as streaked as if I had given birth. I do not have to tell my body what to do; it knows the mechanics much better than I do. As Lewis Thomas said, thank God we don't have to give our liver instructions! I don't have to try to figure out whether to open vessels or close them, or send blood here or there, to clamp off these borders, and open those. No. Thank God, the body knows how to do all that. All I have to do is get out of the way. The mind and spirit can help out with the poetry, the conviction, and the confidence, saying to the body: "I believe in your power, I know you are amazingly strong. I know you want to heal, and I think we can do it." But the actual details of what must be done, of where to send the drugs, is up to the rank and file body troops. Decentralized healing—power to the grassroots!

We do, at times, have the power to move blood, to change our temperature with mental concentration. Yet it is chauvinistic to imagine that the mind knows better than the intricate wisdom of the body and to treat the body as if it were some kind of dull pupil, only semi-competent, who needs to be tutored and guided at every turn.

The role of the mind is not to talk but to listen to the body's requests: "Get fresh air. Eat this. Meditate. Laugh." The body instructs the mind—not the other way around. The mind keeps the overall intention, beliefs, and helpful imagery in place, but the body does the work.

September 5

This morning, back at home, my hair came out all at once. I stood on the deck and pulled it out, thoroughly, tuft after tuft. At first David watched, then he helped. At times he made sad, wistful little sounds.

The tufts—curly, black on one end, frosty at the tips—piled higher and higher on the deck railing. I felt like a ripe milkweed pod as they gently blew away in the breeze. In fifteen minutes it was gone and I was smooth and white once more. I could not take this new appearance seriously. It's a kind of costume change, part of the role. It's not like going bald for the first time. It will take me a few days to remember to wear hats in public, to remember what drafts and slight changes in temperature feel like on bare skull.

Today Debbie told us the game plan: If the gallium scan on Thursday is clean or significantly better, I'll be admitted for a final round of chemo and scheduled for transplant. That puts the transplant in mid October: the time of our wedding anniversary and also the one-year anniversary of the beginning of this saga.

A bathrobe, I think. I'll need a warm comfy bathrobe, and an answering machine to screen calls in the transplant unit. We'll have a transplant humor contest, which I can introduce by telling my favorite joke: "What did the Zen Buddhist say to the hot dog vendor? Make me one with everything!"

Can I do yoga, I wonder, with implanted Hickman lines? Will the nurses let me grow alfalfa sprouts in the windowsill? I'll insist on wearing my own clothes. Sterilize them in the autoclave, I don't care. I wonder if I can wear a Walkman during surgery?

Two owls outside keep singing to each other.

I see David curly-haired and grinning in the rain, David solicitous over omelets, David the playful seducer, David kissing my newly bald head, David my lover, partner, friend, playmate, soul mate. We are so happy despite everything. To be bald reminds me of the spring, a much harder time. But it is not spring, David told me with a smile today.

September 10

In two days, the crucial scan. Even if the last piton breaks, I'm still gripping the cliff, and the climb isn't over. Someone could peep over the edge and drop a new belay line, like a new targeted immunotherapy. No longer do I consider a bad scan, or even a failed transplant, a one-way ticket off the planet. There are lots of chances—lots of possibilities. We found a Chinese restaurant in Gloucester last Saturday, and I received the best fortune cookie of my life: "You will enjoy good health, and live surrounded by luxury."

September 12

Today—calming, sunny, cool air, low tide rising. Up early, organizing and arranging and cleaning. Suddenly, while hanging a calendar, a punch of nausea. Whoa! Where did that come from? "There are lots of things to worry about, aren't there?" sighed David after feeling my tummy. The body's signals are mysterious. Obscure. When I feel a little better, I go on. Neatly printing a list of things to do, I write "Call Keith. Return library books. Stop worrying." What? I do not write the last one down, but it remains etched in the mind, programmed into the fingers until some sort of override operator yells, "Stop! What do you mean, 'Stop worrying'?"

It took enormous effort to walk down the beach, to crawl into a wind-sheltered place in the dunes and collapse, facedown, as if gravity had doubled. That's it! The Earth doubled in mass and I'm the first to notice! This heaviness cannot be wished away. At least I am still bound to the Earth. It's better than flying off into orbit.

Still, I cried in David's arms. We are both braced for bad news on tomorrow's test. The last two gallium scans, the last CAT scan, even the X ray at the end of June all brought bad news. This sense of impending shift is all too familiar. "I'm so tired," I said. "I have been doing this for so long—almost a year."

Just then we were interrupted by a stranger.

"Excuse me," said a lady in a black swimsuit, "Maybe you don't want to talk about it, but I noticed you have the same hairstyle as my husband." She had a friendly golden retriever and two small children in tow. Soon the husband appeared. "Hi," I said to him. "We're talking about what you and I have in common."

Tony was a Chinese-American dentist with relapsed, metastasized head-and-neck cancer. He was scrawny, bright-eyed, and voluble. And how he wanted to talk! For two months he went undiagnosed while his doctor was treating him for an ear infection that was caused, in retrospect, by the tumor. Like me, he had just taken a course of bone marrow growth factor. It was good for him to meet someone who looked pretty damn good after eight rounds of chemo. And it was good for me to meet someone facing a crucial scan with cheerfulness. "Can I give you a hug?" I asked.

"We're members of the same club," he said.

I feel a curious sense of detachment from the body, as if the body has its own life, independent from mine, with its own struggles, its own hidden knowledge. There is a distressing lack of communication, or perhaps it is communication I cannot understand. Is this one of the many languages we have lost? The body knows, even now, all about tumors or lack of them, could sing epic poems about the heroic interplay of forces in the past four weeks. Knows, but cannot, or will not, tell. I tend to think *cannot*, such is the body's generosity and willingness to cooperate. But why this appalling language barrier, frustrating no doubt to us both? "How can I trust you now?" I want to shout at my body. "You didn't tell me what was wrong the last time. How can I trust you ever again?" It is a shout not of anger but great sadness that it has come to this: immense machines and their technicians, speaking like diplomats and go-betweens. We are stuck with imperfect interpreters in place of real communication.

This body—what is it, really? It is both me and not me. It is not me in that it has its own mysterious stories and secrets, and at the threshold of death I will indisputably leave it and go elsewhere. Yet there is the paradox of immanence, the true inhabiting of the body. The body is both I and Thou in the I-Thou relationship. My link to my body is sacred and unique. I am connected to my body as I am connected to no "other." The miracle of incorporation, of owning and loving the flesh. Loving "the actual earth," as Thoreau put it.

Yet, when the chips were down, when urgent communication mattered, my body did manage to get through to me with inexplicable wheezings that may have saved my life.

I'm sitting in the nuclear medicine waiting room. The scans are done, and the results will be given to us any minute. Butterflies. So many alternate futures before me. How to remember the moment before we know, when anything is possible?

September 29

For nearly two-and-half weeks, my writing hand has been frozen. I am like the climber who makes it past the last overhang, finds the crucial handhold, and suddenly is on the ledge, safe. And now, looking down at the overhang and the smooth rock face, she gets scared. "My God, that was too close." For a long time she simply sits on this ledge and does not look up, and does not look down.

I was back in the hospital for five days, getting one more round of chemo. One moment, when the nurses weren't looking, I kissed my bag of iphosfamide. I kissed it. But oh, did it make me sick! Two days I spent squirming, dazed, nauseous, throwing up, managing a few saltines and some ginger ale. I saved my trays for David to eat. The pretty Hispanic dietitian kept reminding me I was not eating.

"I'm doing my best," I said.

"Crackers won't get you up a mountain!" she laughed.

My patience went. "Everyone's been giving me shit around here for not eating!" She was instantly contrite.

But I didn't eat, I didn't do one kneebend, I lay in bed, read novels, and tried to forget my existence. When I was not half-dead, I read through materials for the ecology anthology we are publishing in Russia. How important it is to feel useful. But I could not pick up this notebook. I was still frozen, on the ledge.

I could tell how worried my doctors must have been because suddenly they were so relieved. Debbie threw her arms open for a hug. Arnie paused to pump my hand energetically and say, "I was so glad to hear the good news." He whipped out his transplant calendar, discussing the production schedule as if he were a bigtime film director and I the actress who just landed the big role. Caplan came out of the back room and said, "We're still looking at your pictures—but on the first glance, they look very good." He stuck up his thumb. I jumped out of my chair to hug him. "Wait!" he cried. "I have to finish this first, then we'll talk!"

We saw the scans ourselves. The spots on liver and spleen—gone. The smudge under the ribs, still visible but a little smaller. Everything else cold and clean. *Responsive*—the key word. I am still responsive to therapy. Debbie had hoped the new tumors would shrink—but they actually disappeared! Tak called and left a message of congratulations. They had been worried. Worried as hell. Prudently, they had tried to keep that worry from us. On the ride home as we crossed the Tobin Bridge, I said to David, "I have the curious feeling that in a different reality, another David and Gale are crossing this bridge. In that reality, the scans showed the tumors are growing. They are bravely reshaping beliefs and making the best of it. The separation between us is so gossamer thin, I feel we could reach through and touch the other David and Gale. I am so grateful to be in this reality, and not that one."

We went straight to the beach, danced in circles, chased each other, went out to dinner, slept deeply. The next day, a Friday, I showed up at the hospital to be admitted for chemo. But my sneaky white cells had other ideas and popped out a bit low at 2.8. Debbie wanted to put off the chemo until Monday. I was upset at the delay, but lying under the scanner I realized we were talking about a free weekend, a good weather forecast, and two days of health promotion. We lit out for home, packed the car with camping gear, headed north, and pulled into a campground in Acadia National Park just after sunset. Stars. Trees. The near presence of black ocean.

The two days were a gift, yet I often felt distant, as if I was not really there. Only now can I admit to friends and family just how deep a hole I had been in. Only now can I talk about the one-in-three odds I'd beat. I wrote nothing, except this note: "Gratitude to lichens, to grasshoppers, to pine cones and sunshine, for having made it this far. To the comforting stars, the tough little hemlocks and circular galaxies of ring lichen, to the marsh hawk and brook and crickets and late afternoon sweeps of wind singing across the mountain."

On Saturday night we built a fire, and I kept it burning long after David went to sleep. I needed the solitude, the direct companionship of trees and stars.

I sat looking in the coals and thought: Every fire, every purifying swim, every dance, every song, every letter, every tear mattered.

Who is to say that the prayerful thought from a South African peace activist is not what tipped the balance?

"I'm so relieved," David had said, before rolling over to sleep twelve hours nonstop.

The week before the scan I had three vivid dreams. In the first, there was a shopping bag full of long ropes of amethysts, some pale, some dark magenta, and ropes of pearls. In the second dream, I was in the hospital, playing guitar and singing for some children. My private room was given to someone sicker than me, so I was assigned to a large room where five of us would sleep on a huge communal mattress. I didn't mind; it was cozy and pleasant, rather like a Japanese inn. In the third dream, I was helping a group of Soviet activists, and was surprised to find their office covered with a plush purple carpet. "You have to spend money to attract money!" one of the Russians told me cheerfully. I dream more when I'm well; when I'm ill or drugged, my dreams take a vacation.

At a gem store I learned that amethyst is the most common stone used for healing. I wondered, was there a more powerful stone I might use during the transplant? I was immediately drawn to a small piece of pure cuprite.

It felt warm and alive in my hand. But best of all is to hold it to the light: there are dark flames within like blood flames, bone power, magma, and it made my bones tingle to see them. I was not surprised that its associations are with stimulating the "blood, bones, immune and circulatory systems." I bought it without hesitation. I may not be able to bring flowers or plants into the transplant room but I can bring my stones!

During our equinox celebration, I showed the cuprite to Yuri as we lit the first fire of the year. He also thought of magma—the molten living fire just beneath the crust of the earth—of the marrow, hot and vital, encased within her bones.

October 6

> *Tis grace hath brought me safe thus far,*
> *and grace will lead me home.*
>
> —"Amazing Grace"

Grace has brought us here, to a small corner of New England paradise. The cabin looks out on a wide sweep of cove, and the spruce trees sing in the northern gusts. It is more beautiful than we could have imagined. We've been here only two hours and already feel settled in; a steady fire in the woodstove, a glowing candle by the bed made in the loft. My harvest operation is a mere ten days away. Full-time training on all levels has begun: exercise, calorie stoking, rest. I am putting my correspondence in order and feel ready to start something very new. As I look back over the past four months, I am struck by several things. One: how happy a time it was, despite the cancer. Two: how little guarantee there was that we'd get this far. And three: how hard we worked to earn this triumph. Will and grace were joined to get us here. And now I am in a great position to benefit from this "ultimate" treatment. Surgery, six cycles worth of the drug cytoxin in two days, radiation everywhere, and losing all of my blood for a time. I will be living in a hi-rise womb, totally supported by the care, the vigilance, the nurturing of others. I will receive blood from people I will never see—the commuter on the subway, the store clerk, maybe the woman who yelled at me for running a stop sign, or a big wheel in the Republican party. I know my link to others, to my own species, to this imperfect yet marvelous society.

I cannot imagine the pain and discomfort I will encounter. But what strikes me most is that it won't last forever. It will not be the up-and-down endurance test of chemo, of feeling good only to feel bad again. I'll get all this intensive treatment, and I won't have to do it again. It's finite, and this feels like a great blessing. We give it our best shot, we go to the very edge, and that's it.

I think there is still some lymphoma in my body. Not much, but enough to make it clear I need this treatment. I need this awesome harnessing of the powers of destruction, this full-fledged blast of transformative fire straight from the oven of Baba Yaga.

There's still one hurdle: the results of my bone marrow biopsy. If more than 20 percent of the marrow biopsy is cancerous, that would disqualify me from a transplant. Arnie did a great job with the biopsy. He took out a little snake of bright red tissue, and he exclaimed happily, "Lots of cells!" Everyone says they're confident the results will be fine. The biopsy feels like a bruise, but afterward I ran a mile and walked six, all the way to the mussel beds.

October 7

Debbie's method of coping with bad news is creative denial. "Forget about it. Don't think about it anymore." That doesn't do it for me.

I may still have some very small tumors. But why should I complain about some nearly microscopic disease when the real triumph is that all the old tumors are gone, even before the big-time whoosh? Only one out of three patients with a recurrence gets into transplant shape. Thank heavens Mom never noticed that in the journal article. Only David had known, and we had not spoken of it.

In the daytime now I wear a little amulet pouch with four strong stones: the cuprite, scagilite, moldavite, and "living cross" stone from the Urals. It feels good, hanging beneath my breasts on its thin long string.

October 8

No room for error. One incautious kiss to a sick person, and I would be set back for a month. I must be constantly vigilant. But then the other side of it! The beautiful truth that I am being carried. When I am weak and tired I can relax, and forces working to complement my fierce will and attention will hold me safe. The current will carry me. There is so much grace, if we only open ourselves to it. A vast reservoir of help is waiting across the thin boundary of belief. Open that border just a crack and grace pours in. We are surrounded by love. Only our limited concepts prevent us from swimming in it. Those "in a state of grace" have learned how to stay open, to hold off the moment of reversal when, as Annie Dillard puts it, "the mountains slam." In those moments my overwhelming impression is how abundant grace is, not remote and difficult but near at hand.

This summer's lesson for me is learning to trust in things beyond my own skin, beyond my will and desire. Yes, I can fight alone with my sword of naked will, but it is exhausting. I can also accept help, put down the sword, and rest, cradled and buoyed by the abundant living grace of the world. You might say I have learned how to pray. Or you might say I have learned how to rely on the divine presence within and without. What it comes down to is this: I have learned to take love and nurturance from the beautiful beings around me. When I look at the eagle, when I feel the sunshine, when I hear the pulse of waves on the rocks I recognize this as grace, I name these things as helping spirits. I take them in, and align myself with their healing energy. It is now a spiritual practice. I receive such help, these days, from a lichen.

Campobello Island. I am wedged into a cliff of broken basalt. The sun over my shoulder, a raft of several hundred eider ducks on my right floating on the calm ocean. I have scrambled here to watch the eider, gurgling and cackling and flapping their wings. A little while ago I saw a loon, and before that a bald eagle.

I resonate with the health of this wild place, like a chime humming when a piano across the room sounds a magnificent chord. It is not wild places alone that give help. My own species is full of love, when we get past our fear-boundaries and let it in. Alice Walker and Thoreau and D. H. Lawrence help me very much. Makers of beautiful things help me—even the designer of this pile jacket, of lovely cards, of fine food. Then there is the help we feel, sometimes, behind the full moon's glow, or within the blood red crystal—the help from other realities, other lifetimes, from those on the blue road of spirit, and from places unimaginable.

After the transplant, I must stay open to this help. I will no longer have the obvious moments for prayer: lying under linear accelerators, watching IV fluids drip into my veins, or concentrating as I try to bring a fever down. But there are many other ways to keep the channels clear. I could forget how to do this, but don't think I will. The training has been too thorough, the initiation too tough. And the costs of forgetting very high.

The transplant treatments are purifications with water and fire.

For two or three days I will swim in Cytoxan. I will be underwater much of that time—shapes will be dim, colors vague, with little conscious memory. For two days I will go under, let the currents and whirlpools wash me clean, swirl around me like birth-water, womb-flow.

Then comes fire. The radiation, the furnace of transformation and healing. This fire can kill or heal, depending on how you approach it. With skilled hands, the power can be channeled to protect and spare. All my cells must be given to the fire, to the sharp, burning sword of truth. Courage. It is like stepping into the fiery gaze of God. This fire burns the seraphim's wings—yet the wings are renewed by the flame. And so the loving parts of me, that are in alignment with life, will burn and yet miraculously regenerate. I will be reborn.

Air and earth will be invoked as well. The earth-marrow will be brought to the surface and purified in the air, before sinking back into the holy reaches of the body, in its home soil. And so the ancient circle of water, fire, air, and earth is danced counterclockwise in the banishing direction, moving out of darkness into light.

The Hickman lines are the necessary portals, the places of opening. The arm veins and fingertips have been heroic in their tolerance of IV and pinpricks, but the time has come for going directly in through the larger gates.

All winter, all spring, we were tortured by Bob's backhoe. Bob (not his real name) wanted to cut down all the trees on the island in the marsh and turn it into a manicured garden. "I could have made it beautiful," he told David. He is the same man who began to build an enormous two-story frame house on this island's tidal zone until city officials finally stopped him. The plywood frame is still there, seven years later, severe, and uselessly attached to a tiny cottage. Now Bob is our neighbor, the owner of a patch of hillside covered with scrub birch, oak, cedar, forsythia, innumerable grasses and wildflowers, on a tumbled granite boulder slope. He wanted to make this hillside beautiful. So he took a backhoe and ripped out every tree, bush, and flower. He jumbled the delicate soil layers under backhoe treads, he ripped out long-buried boulders, and got down to bare earth and rock. He then spent weeks rearranging the boulders into terraces, reshaping the landscape until every natural contour was gone. All spring I listened to the clang of backhoe on granite, the fitful growl of the engine, and winced. But he owns the land, and there are no enforced standards, yet, for what landowners may do to their land. Finally the backhoe became silent. Bob rolled in green sod, and trucked in gray gravel, wood chips, straw mulch, and hundreds of nursery-grown petunias. He put in a couple of baby spruce surrounded by sheaths of chicken wire. It is, to my eyes, unimaginably ugly. The suddenly exposed, lichenless, embarrassed boulders are lined up in rows. Were I to mention this publicly, I would be told that this is, after all, only a matter of taste.

Bob was quite disturbed by the fact that all spring we did not mow our small front lawn, and so was Mark, our other neighbor. We enjoyed a lovely procession of wildflowers, free and varied, the effortless gifts of God. Buttercups, daisies, dandelions, clover, spring beauties, and many other smaller and more delicate flowers came and went in a delightful ebb and flow.

"Mosquitoes," Mark said. "You're harboring mosquitoes and ticks in that long grass." Our landlord also expressed his displeasure, but David told him he would not cut the lawn. I think that he decided we were simply a little crazy from stress. Then, just before we moved out for the summer, Bob asked why we didn't mow the lawn. "Did you know," said David, looking him right in the eye, "that if this had been a French colony instead of a British colony, no one would mow their lawns—it's actually only a quirk of history?"

"No, I didn't know that," he replied, startled.

"All spring we enjoyed the most wonderful procession of wildflowers, so beautiful, and for free." With a friendly nod David bid the speechless Bob good-bye.

Our landlord raised our rent fifty dollars this year, and claimed it was to pay Danny, the neighbor boy, to mow the lawn. We now have a respectable crew-cut lawn like everyone else—though it doesn't matter much, since winter is coming.

David is convinced it has to do with a deep distrust of wildness and of Nature, a fixation on cutting her hair, calling her flowers weeds, seeing ugliness where there is natural beauty. How many hours are wasted on caring, cultivating, and clipping these useless lawns? How many landfills are rotting with grass tips? How much herbicide and pesticide caked on loamy soil? How many rivers sacrificed? All for a flat uniform green space that doesn't take attention away from the main thing: the house. A matter of taste? A matter of politics and myth.

October 19

A day like this is a gift from the gods—warm, burnished, restful, coppery, green and gold, with two crows chasing (playing games with?) a redtail who does not even flap his wings. On my Russian calendar, we are in "deep autumn," and I agree.

I have a friend whose life philosophy is founded on the core belief that all of his reality is created by his thought—conscious thought, unconscious thought, and thought from past lifetimes. This belief has helped him very much in his own life, and with it he has successfully helped many hundreds, even thousands, of other people. The beauty of this belief, its scimitar sharpness and usefulness, lies in the notion of responsibility. If we create everything in our lives, if we are responsible for *all* of it, then we cannot be victims. There is not one tiny crack of possibility for victimhood. Since the draw into victimhood can be powerful, it is no wonder that this teaching has benefited so many.

But for people who face a serious threat to their lives that appears, after the most honest and rigorous soul-searching, to have originated *outside* the self, is this belief useful? I think not.

Last June, I said, I realized that if I were holding any beliefs, conscious or unconscious, that were helping this tumor to grow, I had better find them quick and root them out, or I'd soon be dead. Did I want to die? Did I want cancer? Did I not believe I could survive? I had weeks, maybe days, to find out. I searched everywhere for these beliefs. I let my fears take me to very dark realms, lantern in hand, terrified, looking and looking, knowing my life might depend on it. I could not find them, anywhere. Not conscious beliefs, not unconscious beliefs. All I found was a profound willingness to live and belief in the possibility of survival. Yet I kept waking up in the morning and hearing my breath a little more squeezed from the tumor. What was going on here? Was I supposed to submit to the realization, "This is the consequence of events set in motion by my beliefs, in this or past lifetimes," and then become a victim of my own karma? Was I supposed to submit to the realization, "My soul chose this for its own learning," thus becoming a victim of my own soul, or of God, or fate? One might say, "It doesn't matter what past beliefs created this situation—the point of power is the present; you can change your beliefs now, and change your reality now." But this is unsettling. How can you change your beliefs to live, when you can't identify the ones that are killing you? What good does it do to keep reaffirming today the same beliefs you had yesterday, if today the tumor is bigger than yesterday? Unless we can *find* those beliefs that are not serving us, we have nothing juicy to bite into. We are seemingly crippled by *something*, but we can't discover what.

What if we change the framework? What if we say there is nothing amiss with our beliefs, conscious or unconscious, that we didn't *create* cancer? What if we say this came from a force in the universe that operates outside the realm of choice? For example, Coyote the Trickster—the monkey wrench in all universal laws, the unexpected kick, the twist and surprise, the mysterious unlawful *umph* of chaos. Then our energy is not dissipated in a fruitless, self-flagellating search for disabling beliefs. Instead we can focus our energy on *responding* to this force with our powerful choice and will. For this other force is not omnipotent, just as our will is not omnipotent. Coyote can be challenged. He can be overcome. At the very least, the response to him can generate profound meaning.

"But if you do not create all of your reality," said my friend, "how is it that you are not a victim?"

I was thrilled. "A very good question!" And then I answered, "I am not a victim if I stand up and look Coyote the Trickster straight in the eye and say, 'I know what you did—I see it and name it. I know the likely consequences, yet I am going to choose otherwise.' I am not a victim because I do not submit to Coyote. I do not look away from him. I acknowledge him, I respect him, but I also challenge his power. I choose how I respond to his tricks. I do not cede authority over my life. No matter the outcome, I am not a victim, because of the *way* I respond."

To not be totally responsible—and at the same time, not a victim. This was a new thought for my metaphysician friend.

Through his insightful question I began to understand our differences: his universe is one of universal laws that operate dispassionately, of order that can be discovered, named, to some degree understood. Mine is a universe of paradox: "laws" can frequently be true, but are sometimes *not* true; the order of the universe is a paradoxical order, beyond our ability to define in causative statements. It is captured best perhaps by poetry, symbol, story, and myth. There is order, but exceptions abound. There's a cosmic kick, a creative generative mystery as well.

Some advantages of a metaphysics based on universal law are: intellectual order, theoretical consistency, clarity, simplicity, freedom from victimhood. The downsides: dogma, absolutism, tendency toward judgment, a hierarchical ranking of various worldviews based on how well they grasp the "universal law."

Some advantages of paradox: tolerance, humility, freedom from guilt, a better fit with reality and the many contradictory things that are happening around us, beauty, and an openness to learning more. Downsides: a certain fuzziness, a tendency toward easy cop-out answers: "It's all just a paradox anyway." Forgetting that there is *some* order, that we can explain *some* things, or make pretty good approximations: The river does not flow in a square.

My friend Gail says she thinks each person has a personalityless, detached soul, a higher self, which can make choices (such as about living and dying) that are beyond our ordinary consciousness. This force is what I would call the Goddess. And Gail's name for Coyote, I think, is "The Mystery." The question is: What image works best for each individual? What serves us? What helps us? What, for us, sings true?

One week until admission for transplant. Two days—less—until the bone marrow harvest operation at the Deaconness Hospital. On the massage table, I suddenly think: I am the Firebird. And I will be the Phoenix, rising and soaring from the ashes and the fire.

The bone marrow transplant is a modified death. It's like sacrificing an effigy. I do this so I don't have to *really* die. I get all the benefits of death without the inconvenience. Imagine—the learnings of death without having to die, without having to leave my beloved, without losing all the training and experience of *this* lifetime. Well worth the effort. But as whom do I chose to be reborn? What *do* I want to let die, to let go, to toss in the transformative fire? What do I want to keep?

I want to let go of cancer as an organizing principle in my life. There's no question that it *has* organized me; it has had benefits, comforts, gains. Yet I must let go of it. What will be the new organizing principle that replaces it? My work as an artist, the integrity of creation, the act of speaking truth, the wisdom I have earned.

"The presence of fascination," my watercolor teacher called it. As long as I am fascinated by writing, I will keep doing it. That inner, joyful push—that spirit that keeps one awake past bedtime. I want more of it in my life. "For an oak tree to be fully an oak tree is helpful," says Thich Nhat Hanh. I will be helpful if I am fully Gale, a writer-artist, a teller of stories; a prism for the news of the world. All the *practice* I've been getting lately will serve me so well. The discipline of paying attention, the practice of releasing, reframing, letting go. I've become good at it, the way one acquires skill in Ping-Pong or French.

Debbie visits me at 3:00 P.M. I show her the rash. She looks closely, mutters, "Shit," and gets on the phone to Arnie. Now I'm on twenty capsules a day, trying to nurse this troubled patch of skin along. The lesions look *angry*, a deep bright pink, yet thankfully they do not hurt or itch very much. These incidentals would have made my stomach turn a year ago, and now it seems so normal: shingles, conjunctivitis, hemorrhoids, mouth sores, stomach gas, sore throat, cramps, vaginitis, lip herpes, thrush, radiation burn, nausea, sleep disturbance, loss of appetite, constipation. What an amazement general health will be! I'll do cartwheels every morning.

October 20

A magical, blessed day.

Tomorrow is the operation, the harvesting of precious bloodseeds, to be protected and stashed for future replanting. And letting the rest go, letting the field die.

From tomorrow on, I will be scattered. My vitality will no longer be solely within me. I will be splayed forth to the light, to the elements. I will be in pieces—yet all these pieces will be held together by fierce desire. By faith in the future, in renewal and rebirth.

October 22

DEACONNESS HOSPITAL, 6:15 A.M.

It was much harder than I thought. The operating room was bright and welcoming. The three Farber people—Arnie, Zeke, and a technician—masked and dressed in green. As I roll in on a gurney, I wave, "Hello, team!" Arnie reassures the anesthesia team that my blood count is high. The anesthesiologist tries four times to put in the IV, and I almost suggest that Pam come across the street from Dana-Farber to do it. Kathy, a nurse, whispers in my ear that during surgery she'll turn over my Pachabel tape. The anesthesiologist hooks up a tube on my left hand.

Suddenly I seem to be dreaming that a nurse is doing something to my hand. I realize I am slowly waking up. If I am waking up, I think, I must be in the recovery room. This room is much bigger. Many beds. No big lights. It *is* recovery, I think with a thrill. There is the sound of rushing air; I feel the oxygen mask. David appears. I ask him three times to turn the tape over, though, as he explains, the headphones are at my feet. It's over, I think. I just have to wake up. But there are unpleasant surprises. I have to pee. I ask the nurse for a bedpan. Nothing happens. My circuitry is still switched off. The nurse offers me a catheter, says it will bring relief. The catheter burns and hurts. I am relieved the urine is out, but am now in such pain that I gratefully accept a shot of Demerol. When I wake up it is 1:30; I have been there four hours. Finally I am transferred to my room.

I get my own blood transfused back into me. David wipes my dry lips and tongue with glycerin swabs. He reads me *Tom Sawyer*. Between 6:00 and 8:00, I am in a lot of pain. I cannot sit up. Yet they want me to walk around the halls. How? David tells me I have gone eight hours without pain meds and that's why it hurts so much. I notice my wedding band has been taped onto my hand.

October 23

Four holes in my backside, 1,500 cc's taken out. "It went fast and very well," Arnie said. Poor doctors, what a dilemma this is, this damned-if-you-do-or-don't situation. Warn the patient too much and the patient manifests all dreadful expectations. Warn too little, and they're stunned when it's worse than they expected. I had not been prepared to lose my most basic body functions: being able to pee, to drink, to eat, to lift my head, to sit up, to walk. Ugh! I got psyched out, thinking: So this is pain, nausea, confinement. I've only come a few hours, and I'm already near my limits. How will I survive days and weeks of this?

Only yesterday, I felt so strong and buoyant, and now it feels as though every resource has been spent. That's the trouble with pain meds. They affect the mind: You are robbed of perspective. You *have* the inner resources, yet you feel cut off from them.

I don't think anyone can experience general anesthesia without being disconcerted. There was not a blessed clue I was "going under," not the faintest hint of "Here we go!" Just nothing. Memoryless. Click. Could dying be like that? It *couldn't*. Unless there is something to parallel the dreams in the recovery room, the gradual awakening.

What are the real lessons of this humbling experience? That I can't do it alone. That I must ask for help. That I must pray to God and to the Goddess for the strength to endure. I may reach my limits but there are resources beyond me. I must find ways to invite them in. And I must not resist and fight the misery, but let myself be carried by the current.

A big learning, and just in time, too. Just now some person is breathing today's fresh air with thanksgiving, having been released from the transplant room. Just now, that room is being scrubbed in preparation for my arrival.

October 24

AT HOME

A week before Halloween, a week of descent into death. My treatment has been running parallel to the old traditions all along. Still, it was eerie to read the passages describing Halloween in my books on pagan holidays.

> Hallows is the night to turn the Wheel to a new start by descending into death to be reborn. The veils between death and living are thinnest on this night . . . At Hallows, [the goddess] Persephone in the underworld is visited by [her mother] Demeter who pleads for her return to earth. The mother leaves Hecate's death realm with Persephone in her womb, growing toward rebirth at Yule . . . In entering the labyrinth of death on Hallows night, women also enter the womb of reincarnation and rebirth.
>
> —Diane Stein, *Casting the Circle*

> This is the night when the veil is thin that divides the worlds. It is the New Year in the time of the year's death, when the harvest is gathered and the fields lie fallow . . . The gates of life and death are opened; the Sun Child is conceived; the dead walk, and to the living is revealed the Mystery: that every ending is but a new beginning.
>
> —Starhawk, *The Spiral Dance*

I am taking the role of the Goddess. I am becoming her. What does this mean?

Since the full moon, there has been a shift. I have entered a state of prayer, meditation, trance. I feel carried. The descent has begun. My feelings of resistance are gone. I am at peace again.

The hickory and oak on the island are golden light, pure golden coppery burnished light, breathtaking. Hundred of starlings—those blackish, deathly birds—are gathering and flocking in mysterious circuits across the marsh. The wintergreen is pungent. Lichens crisp and dry. Juniper steady and serene. Burnished oak. Windsong. Gulls. I can leave this, knowing there will be return. Persephone: I understand your grief. Leaving is sorrow even when return is promised. I can leave, also, knowing this may be the last sun on my face. This sun, this face.

Is the cancer evil? I have been dancing around this question for months.

Tonight it seems not. Cancer is only disease. Disease is a necessary check to longevity, it's one of the ways the wheel turns: the mold on the leaf, the infection racing through the populous deer herd, the culling to make way for the new. Disease is not evil. Cancer is not evil. If I die of cancer it may be tragic but not *evil.*

Yet I have felt the presence of evil at times. What is its source?

Evil is opportunistic. Perhaps it uses the disease to drive a wedge into our lives. Perhaps it tries to perpetuate woundedness as a response to Coyote the Trickster, while I try to respond to Coyote by loving and creating meaning. Evil tries to use disease to get a foothold in our lives, so that we are tempted to despair, to give up our faith, to dissolve our hope.

Disease itself is not evil. Disease is to be fought. Evil is to be refused.

On the planetary level, we must also fight disease: the razing of forests, the strangling of rivers, the murder of species, the soiling of air, the spreading of poverty. But in our fighting, will we consent to evil by spreading hatred and disconnection through the fighting? Will we win the small environmental battles, but still find ourselves in a state of disharmony and separation? Or will we lose the battle, but in another way win, by fighting and at the same time refusing evil, by choosing to love and create beauty and meaning in the midst of tragedy?

We must do *both*: stay alive *and* stay loving. This is the essence of nonviolence: we fight off the disease, and also resist the temptation to perpetuate our isolation and our arrogance. To stay loving is entirely within our choice. To stay alive is more difficult with our fierce will alone: yet how far, how very far, our will can reach.

Disease is a natural part of the world. There will always be death, sorrow, loss, and grief.

But there is also an unnecessary *wounding* that results from violent acts. Violence is not an essential part to the world. We can reduce it. We can heal it. Slowly, mightily, with love.

Disease and destruction are part of the world, but we have an excess of it. We and our planet are not healthy. We have far more destruction than is needed to turn the wheel of life. If this goes on, the wheel may stop turning altogether.

Evil perpetuates this excess. Refusing evil is essential work. Anything gained by violent methods will result in more disease. But any work that creates harmony, love, and a feeling of connection is a deep and lasting victory. The battle may be lost and the tragedy may happen, but woundedness will be healed, and new patterns will be woven and shimmering.

October 26

MORNING, AT HOME

I put my wedding ring on my altar with candles, sage, and sweetgrass. I wait for the day when David will put it back on. For now, we can imagine it as a golden ring of light encircling us both.

Surgery to implant Hickman catheters was rough. Nearly two hours instead of the predicted forty-five minutes. It is necessary to go back to basics, to remind myself: I am not alone. I am being shown the edge of Mystery. For just a brief moment, in my bath, I felt a surge of anticipation, a spirit of adventure. Not many get to do this—to almost die—and come back to tell about it.

More dreams: I am driving home to Gloucester. A big school bus charges up behind me. I step on the accelerator, start to change lanes, and the steering wheel breaks off in my hands. I put on my flashers and begin to hit the brakes. There is a bridge, a bend in the highway. But all this feels more like a nuisance than a danger.

The Hickman lines are not bothersome, at least not yet. I didn't know how I would feel, seeing four eight-inch long white tubes emerging from my chest. To me, they seem like ornaments, like jewelry. I think of African tribeswomen, their skin embedded with shells and bones, the music of their walk. When my Hickman lines are untaped they dangle with a touch of music, too.

Here's where I can take myself, during the weeks in the transplant room:

- the circle dance in Ipswich
- our bed, under the comforter
- the quarry ledge, looking toward island and marsh
- the woodstove in Maine
- the summit of Mount Elbrus at dawn
- seacliff at Campobello, with loon, eiders, seal
- the leaping whales
- Zhenya's kitchen
- the mussel bed
- the ocean

October 26

EVENING

I am here, in the transplant room, now a sacred space, adorned with pictures of friends, hanging chimes, my amulet bag, and posters of eagles, the earth from space, a medicine woman over my bed.

A friend of David's parents calligraphed a poem from the chapbook I put together last spring, and mailed it to us to hang on the wall:

AS A REWARD

As a reward
the trees stepped closer,
bowed branches, whispered
"It's been too long," then let me pass.

The river hushed and allowed
rocks as stepping stones.
"Hurry," it murmured, "hurry."

Braiding air to show the way
to the cliff, the swallows sang:
"Not only you, not only you."

At last in the silence
of the eyrie, the eagle came home.
"Look in my eyes and follow."

And was gone leaving a feather
to drift from the great nest.

My LDH levels have crept upward again. The lymphoma is simmering, somewhere. So in case anyone thought this transplant was not necessary . . . but no one thought that.

Now, at the price of a couple weeks in a hell made as friendly as possible, I have a chance of returning to full life. Of licking my "incurable" disease. It may be regrowing, but it has no idea what is coming; it has never seen *anything* like this. Five days of relentless bombardment. Every cell washed and burned clean. Dear Goddess, dear God, help these medications to work as well as possible. I want to live; a powerful desire wells up in me tonight! When I leave this room, I will be cured. Free. I *will* this to be.

I dreamed I looked out the back window of our house and saw a wholly new landscape: a grassy trail leading over a hill to a new marsh and estuary full of terns, herons, and gulls. The birds were cold and a bit forlorn, stiff in the cold mud; it was time to move south. Gulls swooped down to peck at eggs left in the marsh grass. The dunes rose to a cliff, overlooking a deep channel. The surface was alive with the wakes of nuzzling fish. Then, to my delight, dolphins appeared in the clear water, leapt together once from the surface, and raced away. They were followed by swift, fabulous animals—a ray the size of a humpback whale, and a giant squid.

How comic that I pulled Opossum from the deck of animal cards today. Opossum's strategy is to *play dead.* Isn't that exactly what I'm doing, to fool this cancer and chase it from my body?

October 27

DAWN

Of course, my old friends, the fear-gremlins, would creep around to visit now, a couple hours before the treatment begins. They whisper, not so loudly as they once did: "You may go through this and *still* have a fast-growing and persistent tumor. What makes you think you will ever dislodge it?"

The immediate, sensible answer is: Many others have done it. The doctors think it's a good shot. If you get rid of *all* the cells, then who cares how rapidly they *used* to grow? The cancer cells haven't a prayer against this new onslaught. They are cheese patties that melt meekly in mere hot sun, that are now about to get blasted in a hot oven for several hours.

That's one response. The other response is that victory is already won. Beauty and meaning have been created. The rent in the fabric has been stitched. If the transplant doesn't work, this will have been my hour of power, these journals will be my legacy. No, voices of despair, I will *never* give into you. I will *always* celebrate. When I feel this truth, I reach a place that is truly invincible. Triumph fills me. The gremlins slink away.

Oh, how worthwhile the battle is—how important to give it our very best try. And to find beauty, even in today.

My hospital room faces northeast. On the Medicine Wheel this is the place of movement from death to rebirth, from endings to beginnings. I will have no sunshine except a brief dawn. This is, indeed, a dark journey across the sunless sea.

November 3

6:00 A.M.

Dreamtime. I have been there for days and come back, but still drift somewhere near its borders. I remember a few, a very few things.

"There is a daughter in danger," I heard the winds say. I heard the winds gather in the north. I felt their dark muscular power. Then they told me about the coming storm: surging tides, gale-force winds ripping the leaves from the trees.

One of those nights, or maybe two, I lay curled under the long, soft, golden brown feathers of an eagle: I so tiny, so vulnerable—the long feathers so strong and soft, so encompassing. I knew what it was to be an egg in the nest.

Now, the hot winds of radiation. Entering the oven of Baba Yaga—the Slavic goddess of death and transformation—bundled and strapped. Entering without fear, by my own choice. And so Baba Yaga took the tapes from my bathrobe pocket and played them loudly: Russian, Bulgarian—magical singing, ancient chants—songs that aligned me as a magnet would, in such a way that my transformation would be *good*. I was aware of the darkened room, the loud whir of the oven, and its square-holed roof. I prayed with every fiber. Let the fire burn clean. Let the fire burn clean.

Then there was another image: I saw myself on a ridge facing a western sea, partway up a cliff. The sky and sea were dark. With me were the Lion and the Eagle. I wore a simple dark cloak, and my long hair was tied back with silver. I stood with my arms forward, palms raised, and listened. I heard the wind and the sea say that by standing up to hopelessness and despair, I had earned a new name.

"You are Daughter of the Four Winds. You are Dancing Star Eagle."

With great gladness, I repeated my name:

"I am Dancing Star Eagle, Daughter of the Four Winds, Child of Moon and Stars and Sun, Sister to all Creatures, Beloved by Singing Sun Wolf, Servant of the Goddess and God, One with the Great Spirit."

The reinfusion of my marrow—my rebirth—was scheduled immediately after the final radiation treatment, a day earlier than we expected. Amy and Rick arrived from Maine in the nick of time and put on yellow gowns. My tubing was wide open. The marrow, a pale rose pink, was running in very fast. David and Amy held my hands and sang blessings to the new life. I had no shaking or chills. It was a beautiful birthing, in all ways. And the closest thing to the joy of childbirth I will ever know.

I like the early mornings, when it is quiet. I'm not so bad today: a full-body itch and a queasy stomach are my only real complaints. I find myself wondering when, and if, the other shoe will drop. I've had a lethal dose of Cytoxan and the same dose of radiation that killed the Chernobyl workers, and here I am.

November 7

Day 7 since rebirth. The new body has been on intravenous food since Monday, luscious bags of thousand-dollar milkshakes. Yet I often feel a gnawing hunger. Eating produces nausea, retching, and cramps of unbelievable intensity and pain. I moaned and writhed for an hour today, as if I were in labor. A few times, my mind began to detach and lift away, but for most of that hour I was spiked into that pain, thrashing, hollering with every breath.

Last night my temperature rose to 101, and the nurses put me on antibiotics. It makes them nervous for people to go to sleep with no white blood cells and no antibiotics in them. Now the fever's over and I have an extensive rash no one can figure out. The mouth gradually worsens and the throat, too, but thanks to the IV food I don't have to eat. I don't think about food when I'm awake, but when I sleep I *dream* about it—sourdough bread, sweet corn, tostadas, chicken with Thai peanut sauce.

I seldom look out the window. I feel no sense of confinement. Every day passed is a triumph. Sometimes I read, or watch "Star Trek" videos, but usually I prefer to curl up in a very light sleep. I think about the canyon country, Russian dachas, curling up with cats, swimming and singing. I picture myself wrapped warm in the writing studio with an electric heater, a cup of tea, and the new laptop.

When I cough my pelvis aches. My skin looks terrible, I still have purple marks going over my nipples from radiation, but I am alive. Every morning I send greetings to the sky spirits and to other beings.

November 8

DAY 8 OF NEW LIFE

Yesterday, I got grumpy with my nurse. I waited a long time for my call to be answered, and when I asked for Tylenol, I was offered oxycodone, a narcotic, instead. I said, "I just need a Tylenol."

"You're having a bone marrow transplant," she insisted, as if I had forgotten. "Most people find the narcotics help their severe esophagitis."

"When I'm in enough pain to *need* narcotics," I cut her off, "I won't refuse them."

David returned and I told him I'd gotten furious. We both started to laugh. "You're getting ornery," he said in delight, "and coming back to life!" Well, if I'd had the strength, I would have hauled off and punched that nurse for saying, "You're having a transplant." How long can I keep up the docile sweetness?

Today I woke stiff, weak, feeling a hundred years old, but something, something seems *better*. I move my tongue. Yes, the whole mouth has been burnt to a crisp, but the pain is slightly lessened. A dental consult dropped in and said, "That ulcer looks like it's healing nicely." Healing! What a blessed word!

I ate half a cup of vegetable rice soup, trying to placate gnawing hunger pains, if that's what they were. And it stayed down. I pedaled the exercise bike furiously fourteen miles in twenty minutes—to Bulgarian dance music. The head dermatology guy came in, looked at the purple patches on my skin and pronounced, "Yeast." All this fuss over diaper rash!

November 10

Dancing this morning—*real* dancing. Kristin, my primary nurse, predicted that today some young white blood cells would appear on my blood count, and she was right. So it wasn't pink Kool-Aid in that bone marrow bag after all!

I prayed so hard going into this, I set up a *form* of prayer which now sustains itself like a persistent mold. The ritual goes on, goes on, I am still between the worlds, in sacred time and space, and will be for many more days.

November 15

DAY 15 SINCE REBIRTH; DAY 21 IN THIS ROOM

Amy offered a homeopathic perspective on the rash: Rashes are often the body's way of bringing things to the surface and getting rid of them. In my case it might have been the Cytoxan—or the lymphoma itself.

Sometimes I am quite perky. I sit up and do needlepoint and listen to Garrison Keillor. Other times I have to nap. The bone marrow growth factor tends to make me "punky" in the evenings. Yet I am proud of the space, the sanctuary, I have created here. Tomorrow I will have been here three weeks. I am just beginning to allow myself to think of going home.

So what, right now, are the take-home lessons?

That the world loves, cherishes, respects, values, appreciates me.

That I'm tough, resilient, patient, and able to suffer and wait.

That I would not change anything I have created in this life.

November 18

My blood counts are coming back very slowly; the changes one day to the next are imperceptible. I weigh 101 pounds. The amount of tubing, bottles, syringes, needles, bags, and other mysterious gadgetry is mind-boggling. So many things in, so many out.

Earlier today David came to hug me and let me cry. I could cry an infinite reservoir of tears once I got started. Tears brought on by pain, by the kindness of my friends, by sheer exhaustion. I have been sick for so long. Yet this morning my body still moved—still moved!—to Olantunji's drums.

I throw up more, eat even less, am on more drugs. But slowly, the blood counts rise.

Curious: The other day I caught myself believing I am thirty-two years old. David had to correct me. I'm still thirty-one. This is how patently I felt I had a birthday when my marrow was given back to me.

November 22

We're on course—the sails are up—but the wind is very, very faint, and we make barely a ripple through these calm seas.

It is not a time that can be easily written about. For now the course is uneventful, one day blurring into the next. Few things change—there are variations in the patterns of calls and visitors, nurses and medicines, sick times and peaceful times, but this is like the variations of poppies within a single golden orange field.

November 24

6:00 A.M.

Oh, the damage doctors can do unknowingly. They call me "slow," call me "pokey." They don't conceal their disappointment about my blood counts. I don't need to be told that my counts have slipped a bit. I need to be told this is normal, average, on course, and given just one word of encouragement. Not these comparisons to others, target dates I keep missing, unfairly raised expectations.

November 27

Today, I found a different way to dance. I danced for a while in my johnny; then, as the drums picked up, I suddenly realized I needed to dance naked. I looked at my body, with its tubes, holes, scars, rashes, yes, but I also saw a slender, strong, beautiful body, with girlish round slim breasts, a dancer's posture, and—this especially amazed me—*strong* arm and shoulder muscles. No weakling am I, under the weakling image of the hospital gown. I could be wearing muscle bras just as well, or fancy leotards. I danced with my hands on my thighs and hips, feeling and enjoying their power. Yes, my neck will always look as though I've spent time in the bone-crushing jaws of some wild animal—but haven't I, after all?

The doctors have grown impatient. They've stopped one of my antibiotics. More radically, they plan to try a different bone marrow growth factor, GcSF, to see if we can't gently encourage (their word is *flog*) my blood-producing cells into higher gear.

Oh, I've pushed myself—getting up half-nauseated to ride the bike, forcing myself to stay awake and up in the chair. But the main battle is going on inside.

November 28

THE ONE-YEAR ANNIVERSARY OF MY DIAGNOSIS

Today, a light spark fell accidentally into the dry brush of fear. Kristen mentioned that my LDH level has risen. She didn't know I knew LDH can correlate with tumor growth. This news immediately opened the door to a great, great sadness. I sobbed and sobbed into my pillow, thinking about this first swallow of failure. The prospect of my early death shook me and I cried until I was exhausted. David arrived and immediately explained that many things can cause LDH to go up, for example, the intravenous food I've been getting. I got reassurance from others, too. Yet I feel weakened by the magnitude of my own grief. How ironic that this occurred on the anniversary of my diagnosis. That first day I did not cry much, but I have learned much about sorrow since then.

Sorrow is as natural and beautiful as joy: It is only right to grieve at the death of a river, or a child, or a worthy idea. It is right—even somehow magnificent—to weep for your own death. In fact, it feels like an achievement. A year ago, I would not have known how to express this sadness. Now I am both drained, and left with a curious peace.

November 29

DAY 29

The emotional release yesterday allowed me my longest and most restful sleep in a long time: seven hours full of dreams about traveling and giving birth to a tiny perfect baby daughter.

Later, I described what the bone marrow growth factor will do for my cells, Gail and David were convulsed in laughter. The growth factor is really an encouragement to my bone marrow cells to have sex. It's the equivalent of honeymoon suites, heart-shaped bathtubs, wine, and caviar—everything to persuade these cells to just *screw* all day and night, asexually, protoplasm spilling off the satin sheets.

Imagine what these cells are going through. First they're sucked out, washed, purged, preserved, put in the freezer for two weeks. Then they're rudely awakened and sent through the heart, with a heck of a challenge to find their way home. When they finally get home, they find everyone else dead. Then the orders come in from the homeostatic mechanisms of the body: Okay, guys, there's only 4 percent of you left, but you have to produce *all* the blood cells for this *entire* body for the next fifty years, so you'd better start reproducing!

This—after what can only be described as a harrowing year. Who wouldn't need some satin sheets, some caviar, and some pampering?

November 30

DAY 30—SATURDAY

Yesterday, at last, my counts went high enough—600 total, 252 polys—that they opened the door to my room. My isolation status formally changed from Stage II to Stage III. Visitors no longer have to wear masks and gowns—only gloves. Rick, Amy, and David were here for the celebration. It was my "hatch day," although I'm still very much in the nest with the other eggs.

Book thoughts. Chapter headings could be: Descent. Paradox. Egg. Hatching. What comes before and after? Don't know; it will come. I'm playing! At last, again.

December 3

DAY 33 (39 IN THIS ROOM)—TUESDAY

A new phase. The GcSF has brought up my white counts. They plan to send me home this Thursday. I awoke after a restless night (they all seem restless now, punctuated with hot flashes) and thought, Soon it will be time to go home. The chest X ray today gave me the heebie-jeebies, as any diagnostic test will for a long time to come. For the first week or so I must come back every day for blood checks, with only Sunday off. But fresh air, our own bed, our own sanctuary will be real blessings. The umbilical cord to the hospital will be tight during the next month of draws and transfusions, a time of waiting, patience, and trust.

I feel I have been so cut off here, so reliant on memory, the *memory* of faith more than faith itself. My Ativanized brain, my continuously complaining body, struggle to remember sunshine, initiative, health, vitality. All these seem to be dimming now, and slightly out of reach.

December 5

After forty days and forty nights I am going home! Only now can I allow these words to thrill me.

Waiting for the chest X ray, I peek at my chart:

"4.96 x 10^7 bone marrow cells." That's what they put back in. Also, an entry on the first day of the bone marrow transplant: "Chest X ray worse than 9/16 but going ahead with protocol despite this."

December 8

The first evening was all quiet celebration and wonder: the coziness and beauty of the house, the fresh green of our indoor garden, a vase of red roses, a long-anticipated dinner of mashed potatoes and peas from Mom and Dad's garden. In the morning, waking to a coverlet of fresh snow, a wreath and presents under the tree.

Yet yesterday was a dark day, with the culture shock of meeting a world not peopled entirely by caretakers and loved ones. All day I had the grimmest thoughts. The days ahead hold new trials. In the handbook they call this "The Adjustment Period." I am coming off Ativan, too, and this should not be underestimated. I had a foul morning in the clinic—everything seemed to go so slowly—and a fever started simmering last night, terrifying me with the idea of readmission to the hospital. I fought it and fought it, tossing under the covers, willing it to go down. It finally did, though it is still 99.4 this morning. I might whistle like a pressure cooker at the least incident. Why does my Hickman hurt when I lie on my right side? Is it the site where one line was removed, or just that I ate too much before bed? Then there are the hot flashes, absurdly, in my left foot. So many things to worry about, and I am mad at myself for worrying, yet I can't seem to stop.

I feel an unease, a gray clammy thing, on my spirit. All I believe in, trust in, have faith in is still there but I cannot touch it. Does it take the most courage of all to reenter the world afterward? What is this restless urge to reinvent my life? I am content with what I have created, with my house, my own beloved things, the structure of my life, yet these things dully oppress me.

PART FOUR

Stepping into a Different Reality

December 14

So reality has, once more, shifted radically under our feet. I had felt such a sense of foreboding.

The twinge in the ribs began Tuesday night during the massage, and woke me up again at 4:00 A.M. Wednesday, as I went through the tests Debbie ordered, I became angrier and angrier. I was furious that such a small thing was being taken so seriously. I confronted Debbie that afternoon and tried to impress on her the importance of positive phrasing. "Do you believe in your heart that I'll get well?" I asked her.

"Let me think about that," she said. I was furious at her hesitation. Why in hell should she have to think about it?

That evening we went to singing rehearsal. Afterward I was very tired, and that night I began to shiver violently. David stacked a mountain of comforters and blankets on the bed; I crawled in and tried to get warm, but it was useless. I could not stop shaking. David crawled in with me but even this did not fully warm me. Suddenly my entire left side seemed to go into a cramping spasm, starting in the pelvis, groin, and leg and extending to my foot and arm. Our next idea, already desperate, was a hot bath. There was some relief; at least I was not cold any longer, but the spasm continued, and I was hyperventilating in anxiety and pain.

The next morning we drove to the hospital. I was ready to fire Debbie if she did not show signs of improvement; I had decided I could no longer stand being around an expectation of the worst. She told us right away: new lesions in the liver. CAT scan today. Appointment tomorrow morning with Peter Mauch for localized radiation to debulk the biggest tumor. She left us alone for a while to let it sink in. When she came back I asked with some of my usual gusto, "Have you given up on me yet?" "No!" she said with a big smile. We hugged each other and I told her that was the most important thing she had ever said to me. Funny, at this moment, I can remember nothing—nothing at all—about the rest of the day.

The next day was inexorably long—meeting with Peter, radiation planning, two bags of blood plus platelets. Yet, I did have a peaceful nap of nearly an hour in the private room in the clinic. If I can go to sleep so peacefully, I said to David, something must fundamentally be okay, and he said, "It seems that on some deep level, your soul is not really panicking." This felt absolutely true to me.

By the time we got home we were both beyond exhaustion. I had chills once more and lay by the heater while David did everything. I felt horrible—feverish, bloated, nauseated, unable to eat the soup David prepared. I felt I was disintegrating and my thoughts became very gloomy indeed. There's facing the imminent possibility of death, and then there's facing the possibility of a great deal of suffering before that moment arrives. Strangely, things improved when I took my temperature and found it was nearly 102 degrees. I got feisty and refused to call the hospital and face the inevitable ordeal of being admitted for antibiotics. I said we were not going to give Debbie or anyone else the responsibility of risking whether or not this was an infection—I myself take full responsibility for knowing it isn't. I said to David, "It's just some combination of estrogen withdrawal, growth factor reaction, systemic lymphoma, and general craziness within my homeostatic mechanisms." I felt empowered and good about the decision. I stripped off my clothes, put a damp cloth on my head, and began to lower my temperature. I cycled through chills, heat, and a sweat that left me drenched. Then I was doing so much better that David left me to go to the store and stock up on Tylenol.

After he left I lit a candle and talked things over with God and the Goddess:

"You know the situation. All I can really say is my life is in your hands.

"There is still hope for a miracle—I have not given up this hope, and I sense from you that it would not be right to do so. It would be a blasphemy to deny the paradox, it would break the laws of humility, to say that I am now sure nothing can save me, and I will die soon.

"At the same time, I must also humbly accept dying as a real and imminent possibility, and make whatever preparations I must so that this, too, can be met with joy and praise. Even as the tears are running from my eyes, even as I feel great sadness and grief at the thought of dying so soon, I must say that I do not feel any large sense of unfinished business in my life. I examine myself for longings, for regrets, for things I must take care of before I leave. Are there places to which I must go, experiences I must have? No. I have been to so many magical places, experienced so many magical things. I have heard the marmots singing to the mountain dawn, I have seen the whales leap, I have stroked penguins, I have taken the resonant beauty of the earth into my body and soul so many times that I cannot say, 'Oh, I must have more.' When I think about experiences with people, the same seems to hold true. So many times I have given and received love! So many times I have felt the thrill of true purpose and meaning in my life! I have stood before audiences feeling the power of my words, I have watched people's lives change, even the world change, and can trace my own part in it like a vein of quicksilver. I have sung with my arms around others, danced and cried out in joy and praise. No, I cannot say, 'My life is incomplete.'

"There was a moment fourteen months ago when I looked in the mirror in Leningrad, caught the eye of my true self and heard her say, with a wise and merry grin, 'You know exactly what you are doing.' On the plane ride home I felt that a sufficient number of my missions had been completed and I really could go at any time. So much has happened since then, yet this fundamental feeling has not changed. I still know I have had the most wonderful thirty-one-and-a-half years of life imaginable. I still love my life fully, and everything I have created within it. I still feel myself to be among the luckiest of people, the most blessed I have ever known. Perhaps it is not possible to have sixty or seventy years of such a life; perhaps it must be condensed into a shorter time. But what, ultimately, does that matter? I have lived many miracles in a short time, and even if there is only a short time left, I could still live many miracles more.

"So as I come to you tonight, your daughter, still my beliefs seem solid as ever. I do not doubt you, or the beauty or meaning or purpose of my life, or of the universe. I will go on singing and shouting praise and thankfulness. You know this. This is my deepest source of peace, the treasure within, what other people call 'courage,' but what I call trust, faith, love for life.

"You know that I love you, and I know you are doing all you can, and I will accept whatever outcome is the best you can devise. You know that I know it is a tough situation, and I will not hold the absence of miracle against you. If it is your will, at last, that I must go, then I will go, I will step into your arms across the threshold of mystery.

"I ask you for strength and help in handling what pain there may be in this leave-taking, and I will give great thanks for every good moment, for every day when I can be conscious and loving, able to love others, to think, to write, to praise, to sing, to talk, to hug and be hugged.

"At the same time I do believe that nothing is written—that it is possible that this enormous challenge has come to me as a final teaching, and that through sheer grace and luck I might indeed go on for some time, and be allowed to write the book, or even books. Who knows? Not even you.

"I am your beloved daughter. I am still here, and I have made my commitments, taken my stands. You know what they are. I am in your hands, and will take what comes with praising and joy. I feel your love, and know I am cradled and cherished. I love you."

I blew out the candle, still crying, but feeling complete, and went immediately to sleep.

It is now Sunday morning. I am not dead yet! I am home on a lovely sunny morning, looking out at the marsh, getting ready for a trip to the beach and an afternoon with Ellen.

I know that it is typical for people to ask, "If this were my last day to be alive, would I be doing something else?" The incredible thing is that I am doing exactly what I would do if this were my last day. I am not ready to abandon the hospital and what help it can offer. I feel tremendously at peace with my loved ones; there is no one, for example, whom I need urgently to see or to whom I need to tell something I have not already said. My affairs seem remarkably in order.

At times I ask myself: Am I grandly fooling myself with this strong tranquil faith? Is there ugly horrible stuff underneath that I am suppressing with all my strength? Is it all just talk? Yet there is evidence that it is truth for me. I sleep peacefully; I drift off into the dreamworld with serenity. This seems a good sign. My feelings are very, very strong, yes, but I can identify them only as grief and sadness—not anger, not resentment, not terror, not despair, not self-pity, not helplessness. I am able to cry freely, at the slightest tender prompting—for example, when I think of the line from "Amazing Grace," "Tis grace hath brought me safe thus far, and grace will lead me home." Or from the song "Wondrous Love," "And when from death I'm free, I'll sing on, I'll sing on . . . I'll sing and joyful be, throughout eternity." It is the same with David. We are present for the smallest poignancy, and it moves through our hearts freely, with nothing blocking it. If I were suffering from an extreme case of prolonged bullshitting of myself, I don't think this would be the case.

What about the books I was going to write? Somewhere deep down, I know I could let those go, too. Especially since I believe David could carry on and become the writer of our team. The most essential wisdom and learnings are safely locked within both of our consciousnesses. He has the talent, skill, and determination to bring them to light in his own form. There are also a helluva lot of notebooks left as reminders and notes! He and I had these thoughts quite independently and simultaneously the other day, and as we sat in traffic on the Tobin Bridge we cried and celebrated these truths. Even if I die quickly, there is nothing very important that would not eventually see the light of day through him. This makes it easier to release the books.

At the same time, why not write what I can, while I can? Yesterday morning in the clinic I was feeling sleepy and weak, and I realized I could easily totter to one side and lay down to rest, admitting my weakness, or I could be stubborn and ask David to get the laptop computer from the car. I said this to him and we both laughed: "It's a microcosm of the bottom line, isn't it?" he said. "Go get me the computer!" I replied. "If I have to, I'll just turn it on and stare at it!" Of course, I did much more. I wrote a four-page introduction to the ecology anthology that will be published in Russia. While writing, I was completely absorbed and happy; I felt no pain or weakness; I was transformed. Seldom have I experienced so directly the mind-body connection. Of course, there are times when the body's pain cannot be so easily overcome. But there are times when it can, and my task is to learn how to become acutely sensitive to the difference between a real need to rest and a false one.

Now I am writing away, telling this story on this new laptop, which I've been using for my journal in the last week. It has seemed too painful to want to pick up the notebook and write in pen, in the same handwriting as before. The computer gives me the sensation of a different voice, a different attitude, that feels congruent with the very different reality we are now in. Interestingly, it is David who, beginning a week ago, has picked up my notebook and begun writing down some of our thoughts.

December 16

IN THE CLINIC, CONTINUED AT HOME

Last night, I told Ellen I do not know whether I am being pulled or kicked into death. It is possible that this simply *must be,* and I am needed there more than here. I also might be shoved out of life by a series of bad breaks that not even the angels can overcome. The angels may be mourning, but also be ready to welcome me, and to say, "It would have been better for her to stay, but nothing fundamental has been disrupted. Her death will bring inspiration and love, not despair or hopelessness."

Ellen asked me what I believe happens after death. I told what had been "transmitted" to me last July by the death-gremlin who had transformed into the white angel of death. The words come back to me now. I must add, of course, that this is merely the imagery that moves my soul. Like any description of the Mysteries, it is at best an approximation, and this one is uniquely mine. I would never claim that it is "the way it is" for everyone.

Death truly is a mirror and reflection of life, the other half of the spinning wheel, the counterwhirl in the spiral dance. When we are on the other side, we are able to choose our way of being, just as we can in life. We can choose the steepness of our learning curves, decide how many risks we want to take, how much effort we want to expend. We continue the patterns and attitudes we have chosen in life, although the crisis and revelation of crossing the threshold gives us an opportunity for a sudden inspiration and a leap to a new level.

Some people believe that dying means becoming unconscious or asleep, and that's probably what they will find. Some choose to let go of their separate self and relax into a universal oneness and harmony. Others fiercely retain their individual souls. Some even choose hell, believing that this is what they have earned. And some choose to become activist angels focusing much of their attention on helping those on this side, the side of life. There are myriad ways of being in death, just as there are of living life.

After entering death, at first there is a great euphoria, as mysteries and truths long forgotten are joyfully remembered and revealed, the relief of leaving the heaviness of the ill body becomes apparent, and we are welcomed with open arms. There is an initial time of blissful rest and relaxation, if we need it. Then come the choices, the opportunities—different than the ones we face in life, yet also similar. We "live" on the other side, on the blue road of spirit. Existence on the other side contains sadness, but the predominant emotions of the other side are great joy and radiance, and blessedness, and the primary activity is praise. Gradually, we feel a longing to return to life. Perhaps we see there is something we must do, a mission we must accomplish. Perhaps we simply find ourselves longing for the smell of flowers, the taste of fresh water, the joining and touch of bodies, the sound of laughter. Perhaps we reach a point where we understand that in order to continue to grow, we must step back into the counterflow of the dance.

Some choose to stay on the other side for a long, long time—perhaps they are recovering from a particularly challenging and painful lifetime. Others plunge back in impatiently, ready for more, perhaps feeling they were pulled away too soon, and the restfulness and peace of death is not a need for them. Others, finding themselves on the blue road of spirit, decide to make the most of it, to glean all they can from that adventure. Some, perhaps, postpone their return to life, realizing they are needed in some way as spirit helpers.

It can be a difficult decision to reincarnate. We are aware of all that we will have to relearn, and the doubts and confusions we will inevitably endure. And we will experience the loss of loved ones. We will forget that we are forever joined to our beloved, and go through the longing and the search for love once more. There are lessons to be learned from loneliness. But we are sure to find our beloveds again, though there is no guarantee of this in any particular lifetime. This is one of the givens of the universe, one of the truths of love—this guaranteed rediscovery of the beloved. And how quickly the memory of separation fades once we are reunited.

This vision of death came to me that day in July, and it still feels solid to me. We spend all of our lives tinkering with this continuing question—What happens after we die? And for all the billions of people who have died, no one can prove the superiority of any particular way of answering this question. It is one of the most personal and intimate possessions we have, our view of what happens after death. All sincere and genuine attempts to describe the Mysteries will reflect some facet of truth. For me, this feels like a whole and complete description rather than only a facet, but I am not the only truth-teller in the world.

David read some of my own words back to me this morning, when I was feeling very, very low. I burst into tears and had a very healing cry. My own words had an effect on me as powerful as that of the poems and songs most precious to me. For this *is* my poetry.

December 17, 1991

AN ELECTRONIC MAIL MESSAGE TO COLLEAGUES

Dear loved ones,

This is a difficult letter to write. Five days ago we learned that my body is again experiencing a major setback. I have several new tumors growing in my liver and a number of enlarged nodes scattered throughout my body. One of the liver tumors is large enough to be causing a number of symptoms, including nightly fevers and pain in my ribs and pelvis. The pain in the pelvis that bothers me most makes it difficult for me to walk (although I still can). I am taking pain medications now, however, and am glad to say that I am doing better than a few days ago.

In short, the transplant did not work. We always knew this was a possibility, but we had of course hoped for the best, and discovering these new tumors only six days after leaving the hospital was a blow, to say the least. My situation is now quite different and we are adjusting ourselves to a new reality very quickly. I must hurry to tell you that I am basically fine, and that on the deepest levels my soul is not panicked. David and I have been engaged in a wonderful, difficult, joyous process of talking, crying, philosophizing, laughing, and grieving. My faith and my belief systems are rock-solid, my life feels well-ordered, with very little unfinished business, and my spiritual bags are packed. Even if I must leave soon, I think I will be able to make myself ready to go. Of course I would still prefer to stay, and as long as life remains pleasant and interesting to me, as it definitely still is, I will do all I can to hang on.

Whereas a week ago, we could assume things would go well unless something bad happened, we must now assume that things will not go well with me (physically) unless something remarkably good happens. But this is the good news—my doctors are quite aggressive and have officially said they are not giving up. The plan is to start me on immediate localized radiation therapy to the liver (it begins tomorrow), which will shrink down the largest tumor and most of the nodes. There are some smaller tumors that they can-

not presently zap for technical reasons, but these are not the biggest concern. The purpose of the radiation is to get me as comfortable as possible and attempt to put me into something closer to remission. The next big step is to treat me with an experimental therapy called ricin. I was supposed to have this treatment anyway in about a month, as a kind of insurance policy, but now we are asking it to do a much bigger job. Statistically it is something of a long shot, but there are several real-life cases of people in my exact situation, or even worse, who responded dramatically to the ricin and three years later are still in complete remission. My doctors are acting fast because they believe it is completely possible that I could become another of these success stories. So I have not been declared "terminal" or any such thing. Still, the facts are plain and we must embrace the essential reality that what will happen next is truly unknown, and that my life is in the hands of God and the Goddess. I may have weeks, months, or years. What is definite is that I have each day as it comes, and that we can pack an enormous number of small miracles into each day. And there is still the possibility that all of these small miracles might add up to a big one . . .

I already feel your complete support and love, and I will love to hear your thoughts and feelings, your reflections, when you are ready to speak them.

Much love,
Gale

December 18

A tough day. But with the grace of God I will survive it.

Last evening, a new and very intense pain began in the area of the tumor, in the abdomen right below the ribs. I went from feeling cheerful to being wholly debilitated, in an appallingly short time. I needed Percocet every three to four hours during the night and in the morning I had to double the dose. If the radiation does not shrink away this tumor, I will not want to be alive much longer, for it is causing havoc on a scale I have never experienced. When I read the previous sentence it seems like an extreme statement, yet I do not think I should erase it, for it really is what I was feeling earlier this morning. I can live with a wheeze and shortness of breath for a long time; but not with this.

Today, we buzzed this mass with a tumorcidal dose. I can hope and expect the symptoms to get better, at least for a while.

I have a tough decision to make—whether or not to give up my singing group's performance tonight. I am beginning to realize it is totally unrealistic. I cannot take deep enough breaths to support song. The sharp pains come, my lungs are pressed, my respiratory rate is too high. I am afraid that even strong drugs could not get me through. Part of me says: "Do it anyway, for the sheer craziness of it. Even if all you can get out is a few yips and yodels." Another part of me says: "This is absolutely, utterly absurd. You might fall over in the middle of the performance." It seems worth reflecting upon, that in less than a week I have lost the ability to do two of the things I most love to do in the world: dance and sing.

The other decision is whether to take Debbie up on her offer of a continuous morphine infusion. I am not thrilled with the notion of being wired full-time or wearing a battery pack. But I am being humbled, quickly, by the intensity of this new pain.

December 19

Moments after we arrived home from the clinic, Rick and Amy appeared. A complete surprise. They showed up with a Christmas tree. Thinking we would not be home, they had the nutty plan of sneaking in, decorating the tree, and leaving it for us to find. Instead, we had a chance to reminisce, to play with two-year-old Emma and get her advice about boo-boos, Band-Aids, and noodles. When the morphine pill kicked in, I thought I would collapse, but the distraction of decorating the tree brought me back. What a life-filled evening! We were singing Amy's lyrics to the tune of "Amazing Grace," resurrecting the "Cancer-Fear Blues," remembering how to be joyful and trusting, silly and celebratory.

I slept well that night, but not enough. So the next morning at the hospital while waiting for a transfusion, I slept two more peaceful hours on the couch in the lounge.

December 22

I am working so hard to open myself up to the miracle of solstice, to the possibility of turnaround, to the belief that I have passed through the time of greatest darkness.

Yesterday was the worst day I have ever experienced. I began feeling fragile, weak, tired, and then had an unexpected reaction to the platelet transfusion—high fever and racking chills. I felt utterly stripped of my mental and spiritual resources. It was the closest I think I have ever come to despair. It was as if my entire being was in retreat, and wanted only to retract from the world. I dreaded any kind of outside stimulation, even the sound of my beloved's footsteps coming up the stairs. So it took all my strength to greet our friends who came for a solstice gathering. After the beginning of the ritual, I excused myself and went to bed, at 6:30 P.M. As I lay shivering and stiff in bed I prayed to go to a place of beauty and rest, to be given some relief from the day's unrelenting discomfort and discouragement. I was able to nap peacefully for awhile but then woke to uncontrollable fevers and a temp of 102.4 on Tylenol. My pulse was racing at well over a hundred, and I felt I would simply burn up at this rate. Then suddenly, around 4:00 A.M., my body cleared and my outlook shifted. The relief was overwhelming.

The first small miracle: My platelet count is 20—it has gone *up!* This is major news. I must be beginning to make my own platelets. Hurrah, little megakaryocytes! You could not have picked a better moment to come through. Once my platelets come back to normal, I can get the experimental ricin treatment, which offers a long-shot chance, about one in eighty, but still a chance. And in the meantime, today I don't need a transfusion—we can go *home!*

The great lesson: Even if I am in a place of despondency, wonderful things can still be happening. Moods do not block miracles.

How nice it is to be let off the hook of responsibility for constantly visualizing the positive. A whole network of friends, loved ones, bodhisattvas, and angels takes over when I go off duty. It is no longer my role to carry the ball. I don't have to carry anything. When I say my life is in the hands of God and the Goddess, I mean, among other things, that my life is in the hands of the many people who are on full alert, who are working magic, directing energy, hollering, crying, arguing on my behalf. I have angels on the other side doing their darnedest, and I have people-angels on this side doing the same. I can let go and trust in their magic. I don't have the primary responsibility for this; not when there are so many other burdens that only I can carry. Volodya Shestakov, as usual, summed it up wisely in an electronic mail message from Leningrad. Special cosmic healing energies are available several days after solstice, he said, and many people all over Russia will be directing these energies toward me. Then he said: "Please rely on us and expect recovery." Nice and straightforward. Lean back, relax, and we'll care take of it. I like it!

December 24—Christmas Eve

Last night I went to bed expecting a good night, but instead had a difficult one. A new symptom, a positional cough, became too regular to deny, an old warning signal of chest trouble. Then I began to hear crackling sounds in my lungs. The faint beginnings of a wheeze. The idea of the chest tumor returning gripped me and would not let go. I became anxious and could no longer find that restful place within. Today's hospital chores exhausted me, and after the transfusion I had to rest for thirty minutes before I could imagine walking to radiation. Then David heard that the chest X ray indicated a pleural effusion, some moisture leaked out of the lungs, which is typical for a transfusion reaction. Suddenly we had a far nicer explanation for the positional cough and the crackling sounds.

Rick and Amy were waiting for us when we got home. I spent as much time with them as I could, and then went off to bed. I worked to control the fevers, and succeeded; at one point I even slept five hours in a row. At another point I woke up from a strongly affirming dream in which medical people told me, "You *are* getting better." One clear sign is that I can sing a little now. The pelvic pain has faded to a whimper. The ribs are better. But then, the liver has been quite tender, and my whole abdomen feels enlarged.

I am still trying to work through the disturbing realization that when the chips were down and I was *really* sick on the evening of the solstice, I could not access my source of spiritual comfort. I felt like I was dying, as if I were disintegrating on the spot, and nothing seemed to lift my misery or bring a sense of merciful relief. Here's the kicker: If it's this way now, when I probably am not dying yet, or have only just begun, what can I expect later on? Will my beliefs be unreachable when it really counts? Will the presence of friends be something to recoil from rather than embrace?

Fortunately, I can see another side of it. When I finally *let go* of wanting to participate in the solstice ritual, when I called it quits, went to bed, and prayed to go to a place of beauty and rest, then relief came almost *immediately*. When I gave up, a space opened for mercy. This bodes well for the future. The dying process can be merciful, I think, if the call to retreat from life and seek healing and rest is followed, not resisted.

Wednesday, December 25—Christmas Day

And so what is one to do with the fierce will, the stubborn statements of hope, the passion and desire to live? What is one to do with the habit of being a warrior, of embracing the paradox, yes, but primarily focusing on choice and will? All of this activated desire is like a bag of treasures hanging heavy around my neck. I must summon the strength to remove it. I do not wish to deny my choices and desires. That would be giving up. But I must set them aside, for their heaviness is too much of a burden to me now. They still exist, they continue to act in the world. Only I cannot carry them now—others must.

I am such a warrior, by habit and nature; there is no way that this aspect of me is going to fade quickly. Even if I spend all of my energy on trying to release, the warrior in me will keep going on automatic pilot. So I needn't worry that in letting go I am abandoning choice or determination.

Gail said she thought I might be in the process of making a deep decision about whether to go or stay. I immediately replied that this is not the place of decision for me. I made my choice to stay many months ago, and it is still unwavering. My hand has already been played, my cards are already on the table, my preferences loudly stated; now many other factors and forces will come into play and eventually there will be an outcome. My preferences are a very important influence, but there is no mystery about them, whereas there is plenty of mystery about the other forces going on here.

No, my place of decision is elsewhere. What I must now decide, and put into practice, is *how* I am going to keep going through this process. It is incredible, how steeped we are in the notion that dying is bad, living is good, death is a failure, cure is success. It is the same paradigm which judges the value of your work by how much money you make. It is the same paradigm that says the world is dead, matter is unconscious, and we have only a little blip of linear time before death puts an end to everything. It is the Cartesian paradigm that destroys forests because they are nothing more than lumber. It rejects the natural cycles, the fluidity between worlds, the mystery. It rejects, of course, the Goddess and all she represents.

Though I know this attitude toward death is destructive, still I find myself weighed down by it. These ingrained assumptions about death are everywhere. They dominate the medical field, and I am spending seven to eight hours a day in hospitals. It is *very* hard to break out of them.

David and I have to stop obsessing with the details of symptoms and blood test results. We have to set the medical stuff aside. We had a few hours this morning of genuinely not thinking about it, and they were wonderful. I have to go ahead and die, in the sense of vividly imagining my death, accepting it, loving it, losing my fear of it. Only then, perhaps, can I imagine stepping back over the threshold, of discovering, to my surprise and delight, "It is not yet time."

On the drive home after visiting us, Rick and Amy asked their two-year-old daughter, "Emma, what do you think of the spirit world?" She thought about it for a long time, then answered in one clear sentence: "The moon helps the spirits of people learn how to play."

I had a vivid dream last night of Danite pressing her foot on my body and giving me an exercise: "You have twenty-five minutes to name the people with whom you would like to have an experience of complete, open, whole-scale unity of consciousness. This experience will be made available to you soon." I woke up as a stream of names burst into my mind. It is a good question. Whom do I love enough to want to have them know all of me, and me all of them? With whom do I have that kind of trust? From whom have I no secrets? Who has treasures and secret realms I would be privileged to explore?

One of my challenges is coping with simple sadness. The bare fact is that this was *not* my first choice. Things are not working out the way I have wanted them to. I would still prefer to have the extra time here. But, in the end, how much does it matter how many years we live? Was Grandpa Warner's life more filled with inspiration and beauty than mine, simply because he lived three times longer? I am not sure that it was. To believe that the value of a lifetime can be measured by years is to buy into a quantitative, linear view of the world.

We do the best we can with what we are given, and I have been given plenty. It is not selfish or demanding to ask for more, but it is also not a cry of desperation or regret. I am used to getting my way and it is a shock to not be getting it. But this is my work—this true releasing what I desired, and opening to the possibility that, for reasons I can and cannot imagine, it may be best that I go soon. It has occurred to me that I may be given the opportunity to go while my inner peace is so beautiful and strong. Dying gracefully now is a real possibility. Who knows what suffering I am being spared?

I need to collect small mantras and sayings, to surround myself with the music and the books that comfort me and make me say "yes." It is hard to know what to do with the accumulated talismans that were so filled with hope such a short time ago. Should I go on wearing my amulet, or my amethyst? Perhaps I need to lay them aside as an indication that I am putting down my warrior's tools and stepping into a different reality.

December 26, 1991—Thursday

So, is it possible—that this could be *it?*

The details seem to fit. My breathing is rapid and labored even though I am wearing an oxygen mask. I am on a stretcher in the clinic. They want to admit me. My temps are high, and this morning reached 103.7. And now they say the chest X ray looks much worse than two days ago. They think this havoc is being caused by lymphoma itself in the lungs and chest. Which we cannot do a hell of a lot about.

I am still alive, but I may be dying, and it may be soon.

Oh, there have been times, in the nights, when listening to my breaths I have known! When the profound weakness in me, the coughing, the shortness of breath, all whispered this to me. Yet this news is still a surprise.

Gale dear, are you ready for this?

On some level we can never be ready, perhaps. I am not as ready as I hoped. I had thought I would have a little more time, if only a few weeks. Yet we must take what we are given, and there is something to be said for going fast.

Everyone says that when the moment of death arrives, there is no fear, only joy and anticipation. It's the getting to that point that can be hard. It's possible that I'm not yet near enough to the true release to be able to see and feel its gifts. It's possible that things will only become easier from here.

I recall, so vividly, the times I thought, with a shiver, "Even if this were all we had, it would be enough." I remember this coming to me while sitting next to David on the quarry ledge in a cool, twilight rain last May, just before we discovered the first recurrence. It has come to me many other times, in settings of ecstasy, when I felt a gentle touch through the veil.

David comes in while I am writing this, after calling my family, and tells me he feels joyous. I am not far from this myself. It is a beautiful day to die, after all. If I can cherish and praise my dying, there will be less to fear.

Of course there is nervousness about the unknown, about embarking on an adventure one is sure will be wonderful, but whose details are obscure. I feel a little like I did landing in the Soviet Union for the first time by myself. That, also, took trust. This is trust on a far bigger scale!

Yes, I think I have already died, several times over, and we have already had a number of respites and grantings of more time. We may have run out of extensions. But look how far they got us! Down all those rivers and up all those mountains, that idyllic week in Maine, these last visits from friends, and blissful massages. I can call it enough. I can even feel, within my spirit, a restlessness and willingness to go.

Dying at home versus the hospital? I think the setting is not so terribly important. The process seems far removed from such details. I have felt fresh air on my face, I have seen the marsh, I have slept peacefully in my own bed, I have touched the ocean so many times, I don't feel the craving for more. More important are the flowers, candles, music, and loved ones. And giving David a rest. Coming to the hospital can be a way for us to accept help.

What can serve me most?

Reading inspiring poetry and passages on death and dying, or having them read to me.

Listening to my very, very favorite music.

Seeing and talking with a few very, very special people.

Making a list of my experiences with deep spiritual meaning, so that I can quickly call them to memory.

Afterword

We spent Christmas day at home. Gale put her notebooks in order and showed me where she kept them. We watched the video of our wedding of four years before, which we had never seen.

That night she was breathing rapidly and I could hear the sound of moisture in her lungs from across the room. At about three in the morning, despite racking chills, she managed to comfort me in my grief. She thanked me for taking such good care of her, and wondered if she would have been able to do the same for me.

When I emerged from my morning shower I was amazed to see her downstairs, dressed and sitting by the door, ready to make the daily trip to Boston. After her radiation treatment, she walked through the hospital to the meditation sanctuary, now as familiar to us as our own living room. She looked so ill that I asked a nurse to bring in some oxygen. After they took her on a stretcher to the emergency area, I left to telephone family and friends and tell them it was probably time for them to come. I relayed Gale's request for people to give, on her answering machine, positive messages about dying, and to say what was exciting in their lives and what they were doing for the planet, since Gale envisioned herself becoming an activist angel, able to assist from the other side. When I returned, Gale was sitting on the stretcher, wearing an oxygen mask, writing on her laptop computer her last journal entry.

"I feel nervous about the passage into death," she said through her clear plastic mask. "Nervousness, more than fear. There's a distinction!" There was a certain triumph in her eyes at this.

Her hospital room turned out to be next door to the sanctuary, so when family and friends arrived the next day, we brought in the chairs from the meditation room and made a circle around her bed. "We're bringing the sanctuary in here," I announced. "And I'm the flowers on the altar," she quipped.

Amy asked Gale if she had any ideas for the memorial ceremony. "I'm sure you'll do a bang-up job," she replied.

Later, Gale suddenly said to her parents and brother, "Make sure and welcome David's next wife into the family," and added, "He obviously has good taste."

It was a long night, with a painful chest tube and enough morphine, finally, to relieve the pain. The bedside vigil continued through the night, her father holding her hand. "When the time comes, I will release," she whispered. During the night our friend Laurel sang a Russian lullaby. Then Gale said, "Here's one you have not heard," and starting singing in Russian but soon ran out of breath.

In her sleep, she was panting at an incredible rate, as if she were in labor. Instead of pushing out a baby, she seemed to be pushing out her spirit.

In the morning a shaft of sunlight beamed onto her bed. Gale opened her eyes and was delighted to be surrounded by a ring of family and friends. We sang "Lord of the Dance," and then "Wondrous Love." She and I whispered words of parting, "but not really good-bye." We sang "Amazing Grace" and she mouthed every word beneath her plastic oxygen mask. Then she murmured, before drifting off again, "Good-bye everybody, I have work to do."

While she slept, a friend sang a song about the timelessness of the ocean and the wisdom of the forest. It was an exquisite song we had never heard, and the moment it finished, Gale's breathing pattern shifted. Now her body seemed to be breathing on its own, without her.

Eventually, the rapid breathing began to wind down. At 12:55 P.M., three hours after she had sung "Amazing Grace," her body rested quietly. After such a long struggle with fevers, she felt so wonderfully cool.

Acknowledgments

The first year after Gale died, I told people I was editing a book. What I was really doing was sitting each day by the marsh, savoring a few pages at a time, hearing Gale's voice in the words, sifting through our life together. Our final year had been a whirlwind, yet here was life recorded, details laid out in order. I would sit for hours, letting the words trigger images and memories, and with each new memory, waves of anguish. As the months passed, I was more and more able to see, without tears, the whole tapestry of our relationship, admire its beauty, and gird myself with its teaching. And so, my first thanks in these acknowledgments go to Gale, whose living voice supported me in my grief even after she departed.

Gale's journals were private. Three days before she died, she asked me to take four thick notebooks off the shelf and bring them over. "I think it's time I gave these to you," she said. She knew I was determined to turn her journal into a book, and she was glad that, though I could never write the book she had planned, at least I might be able, as she put it, "to rescue some of it." I opened the notebooks and looked at what until that moment had been forbidden territory: nearly a thousand pages packed with her tiny script. I felt overwhelmed by the reality of tackling it without her. "Don't try to do it all by yourself," she said. "Get help."

It was good advice, and once I was ready to get down to work on the manuscript, I took it. People stepped forward to offer support in many forms, and my heartfelt thanks go to Louise and Jack Warner, Ellen Wingard, Geraldine Gomery, Gail Straub, David Gershon, Amy and Rick Donahue, Bernie Siegel, Susan Roberts, Ned Leavitt, Jerry and Sara Kreger, Jonathan and Val Kreger, Jennifer Kreger, Wade Gray, Gerry Camarata, Jennifer Doble, and many, many others. Special thanks go to:

- Dan Gunther, for being among the first to believe in the importance of this book;

- Val Petro, for deciphering hundreds of pages of handwriting;

- Martha Collins, for stewarding Gale's poetry and naming the parts of this book;

- Cynthia Lazaroff, for believing in the possibility of the best and providing stalwart support year after year;

- Joan Marler, for helping clarify Gale's references to the goddess;

- Valerie Andrews, for lovingly and masterfully pruning the original manuscript and being an all-around angel of support;

- Elizabeth Pokempner and Muriel Nellis, for ably shepherding the manuscript into the world; and

- Laurie Abkemeier, at Hyperion, for graciously adding the finishing touches.

Very special thanks go to Ronit Bodner, for contributing to my feelings that Gale's spirit, her family, and this book are so welcome in our home and in our lives. After a six-year journey, the book found its home at Hyperion one week before our wedding.

GALE WARNER (1960–1991) worked as a freelance environmental journalist for various publications, including *The Christian Science Monitor*, *The Boston Globe*, *Parade*, and *Sierra*. An accomplished poet, she received the American Poet's Prize in 1985. Her poetry has appeared in *Agni*, *Gaia: A Journal of Literary and Environmental Arts*, and *West Branch*, among others. She authored two books about ordinary people helping to end the cold war, and cofounded Golubka, a nonprofit group in the former Soviet Union that supports social activists with publications and training. Gale also worked with children as an environmental educator, and helped her parents to found the Stratford Ecological Center, which fosters a deeper relationship between people and the land though experiential education in ecology and sustainable agriculture. Gale completed her undergraduate work at Stanford University and received her master's degree from the University of Massachusetts, Boston.

DAVID KREGER, M.D., is a Harvard-educated physician who leads workshops on leadership and empowerment, and develops social initiatives on the growing edge of culture. He has delivered over two hundred presentations and workshops throughout the United States and the former Soviet Union. David partners with his wife, Ronit Bodner, Ph.D., to coach individuals and families, and co-lead workshops on themes that are kindred with this book. He lives with Ronit and his stepdaughter, Shir, in Lincoln, Massachusetts.

David and Ronit enjoy hearing from readers and warmly invite you to inquire about their workshops by writing on e-mail to DKreger@aol.com.

Gale's book of poems, *Breathing the Light*, is available by sending $16.50 (checks or money orders made out to The Gale Warner Fund) to:

David Kreger
P.O. Box 6182
Lincoln Center, MA 01773–6182